E-Commerce for the Clueless®

Mike Rounds

E-Commerce for the Clueless®

CPMPub@RoundsMiller.com

This book contains excerpted copyrighted material from *Fishin' With A Net™ 8th Edition, E-Commerce for the Clueless®, Self-Publishing for the Clueless®, and Trademarks® and Copyrights© for the Clueless®.*

Disclaimer

This book is written with the understanding that the author was not engaged in rendering legal services. The information included has been carefully prepared and is correct to the best of their knowledge as of the publication date. If you require legal or expert advice, the services of professionals should be used. The author disclaims any personal liability, either directly or indirectly, for advice or information presented in this book.

The information as described has been used successfully to obtain profits for some of the people who have used it. Although all efforts have been expended to supply the latest in complete, accurate and up-to-date information, it must be understood that the ultimate success of the user is dependent upon market conditions, efforts expended by the user, and other variable factors that are beyond the control of the author, and that neither the users' actual expenses nor successes are guaranteed nor implied.

Throughout this book, trademarked names are used. Rather than put a trademark symbol after every occurrence of the trademarked name, the names are used in an editorial fashion only, and to the benefit of the trademark owner, with no intention of infringement of the trademark.

At the time this edition was printed and released, all of the sites listed were active and accessible to anyone having access to the Internet. Neither the author nor the publisher is responsible for broken links, abandoned sites, or changes that are beyond their control.

Contents

Introduction

Welcome to the world of e-commerce, the hottest and most talked about business opportunity in the world.

E-commerce is being so loosely spoken about nowadays that people tend to be apprehensive about what it actually entails.

For example, can you really make all that money in it as the marketers claim?

The answer is yes if you go about it the right way.

According to *International Trade and Investments News*, the largest driving force in the global economy is now e-commerce. By changing how we buy, and from whom, the marketplace connects consumers in the most populous countries of China and India to an entrepreneur in Los Angeles or New York with an idea, a product, and a laptop.

According to Census Bureau estimates, e-commerce sales in the U.S. passed $263 billion in 2013, up almost 17 percent from 2012!

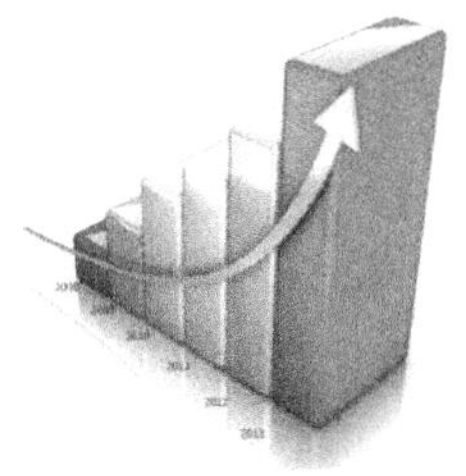

E-commerce is getting faster and smarter, but it still relies on the entrepreneurial spirit of individuals who want to get involved with the process.

That innovation over the past four decades is perhaps best illustrated by China, whose growth in e-commerce specifically has been nothing short of meteoric.

China is now the second-largest e-commerce market in the world, with online sales of $125 billion in 2012—and it is soon to be the first with expected sales to reach $270 billion by 2015.

Resources for A Successful E-Commerce Career
Courtesy of the Small Business Association

Obviously, you're looking into e-commerce so before you go any further, there are some basic things to look at, including some highly informational web sites, before you take the plunge.

Practical e-commerce – This is a nice blog which provides down-to-earth articles and advice to help smaller businesses succeed online. It is useful no matter your e-commerce experience or the size of your online store. (www.practicalecommerce.com)

E-commerce bytes – Blog similar to practical commerce but with more interviews from leading persons in the e-commerce market. They post articles each day. (www.ecommercebytes.com)

E-commerce ABC – A practical e-book describing the whole process of creating an e-commerce business, starting with how to create it and how to get more traffic and sales. Although it's not free, a lot of information is available on their Web site and in the free preview version. (www.abc-of-ecommerce.com)

Powersellersunite.com – Very big place where many online sellers post useful information, tricks, how to's, etc. very useful for any online sellers, especially for those selling on online marketplaces. (www.powersellersunite.com)

Get Elastic – As they claim, the #1 subscribed e-commerce blog. Just like Practical commerce and E-commerce bytes, publishes daily articles with useful information related to e-commerce. (www.getelastic.com)

But hold your horses, cowboy. It's not as easy as it looks.

Before you get yourself tangled in e-commerce, here are a few things you should know first.

You may have read about the new generation of tech millionaires under the age of 30 and wondered if it was time that you got yourself involved with an online venture yourself. Won't that be great?

Being your own boss, calling all the shots, go golfing whenever you feel like it, and charge all your trips and meals to the company's account. That's the life!

It Takes More than Just An Idea

It seems so easy to get into an online business nowadays.

You can just take a successful and working business concept, tweak them a little, and add an extra feature or two, then market the business out as your own.

There are people who do that because... why mess with something that works, right?

But don't think that you can piggyback on the pioneer's success if you are going down this road.

A lot happens behind the scenes.

You can't see the inner workings of the organization, the amount of time and effort devoted behind marketing, and finding and retaining good staff; the dedication it takes to provide customer satisfaction and handle difficult requests; etc.

What I'm trying to say here is don't think that just because you know the idea works, you can leave every other aspect of the business unattended, because that is pretty much one of the main reasons a business will go bust.

Money Isn't Easier To Make Online

Based on my years of experience, it isn't as easy to make money as the hucksters would have you believe. Period.

Before your business can hit the skies, you have to first spend quite a sum to get it down the runway and take off first.

We're not talking about a freelance business where all you need is a platform to market your expertise (a blog, a self-made website or a social media network), a portfolio to showcase your talents and strong networking ties.

We're talking about the cost, time and effort it takes to get a team together to work the areas that make the cogwheels in your business run – things like the setting up of a content management system, and payment solutions that will give your customers the confidence to do business with you.

Having round-the-clock technical support will also be beneficial to the business since there is no closing time on the Web.

Also equally important are the branding exercises in social media networks.

All of this will take up your time; if you don't have the time, you still need to pay someone else to do it for you.

There's A Lot of Commitment Involved

As I'm sure you would have realized by now, there is a lot of commitment involved if you want your own e-commerce business.

As with any other life-changing event in your life, having your own online business will also affect your current lifestyle.

All that talk about being your own boss means you can get on and off work as you please, right? It doesn't work like that.

You may be your own boss, but you answer to customer demand.

For starters, you can throw your weekend plans, shopping trips and movie nights out the window because you're not going to find enough time to eat a proper meal.

Anytime you aren't manning your counter, you may be losing out on a deal to a rival.

Getting someone else to watch the counter for you will cost you, but you really don't want to burn out before the business takes off, and it will take a while before it starts to simmer.

But what really sucks about being the man (or woman) on top is that you don't get to call in sick to get away from all the madness no more.

- Have a busy period? Deal with it.
- Got a tough customer who just won't let you get your way? Suck it up and deal with it.
- A client or supplier reneged on something promised to you? You guessed it. You want to be the head honcho, you deal with it.

The Stress of Decision-Making

After the first hurdle, you may have made a name for yourself and with things going so well, you may be thinking of expanding the business.

Here is when your analytical skills and decision-making skills may help you make or break the business.

As your business starts to build up, you may consider investing in new technologies or hiring new, or more, people to help you watch over things.

However, if you expand too quickly, you may find your liabilities locking up your cash flow, and over time, it may drag the business down like an overzealous anchor.

Expand too slowly and you may find your staff (or even yourself) overworked, customers running off to a more efficient rival and no one happy.

It's a precarious spot to find yourself in, this balancing act between low-threshold stability and potential high income risk, but it's a stage you want to look forward to because it means that your business is doing well.

The stakes are higher on the Web because users don't respond to changes lightly. But that is a risk online entrepreneurs may have to face to take the business higher.

My last thoughts

I'm not trying to deter you from engaging your own e-commerce experience.

However, we do want you to know what you are getting yourself into. Starting your own business is not something you can turn on and off like a light switch.

And it's not like school, where if you study hard you are likely to get a good grade. At times, if you spend too much time trying to perfect your craft, your online business may lose out on new upcoming trends and be left stuck in the mud.

Nonetheless, if at the end of the day you find that e-commerce is not your cup of tea, you can always choose to sell the business to cut your losses.

10 Tips to Skyrocket Your E-commerce Business

Assuming that you've decided that e-commerce is what you're committed to, we want you to know that there are hundreds of thousands e-commerce shops inundating the internet. Some sites skyrocket, some stagger, while most of them sink without a trail. That makes us wonder what makes an e-commerce store successful.

We have found ten essential factors that significantly contribute to the success of an e-commerce business and will help it be successful faster:

1. Sell only those products that fetch higher margins
2. Sell products that grab eyeballs
3. Learn online marketing with special focus on search engine marketing
4. Attract advertisements
5. Hire an experienced Web developer
6. Keep adding more and more products to your store
7. Write good descriptions and upload better pictures
8. Ask customers for product reviews
9. Bank heavily on SEO
10. Spend money only if you are assured of returns

More Tips from the SBA about E-Commerce

According to US Census data, e-commerce sales are increasing at a rate faster than traditional offline retail sales, raking in approximately $190 billion in sales in 2011.

So it's no surprise that budding entrepreneurs and existing "bricks and mortar" businesses are turning to e-commerce as a business opportunity.

You only need to browse the SBA.gov Community Discussion Boards to see how many topics focus on how to start an e-commerce business!

If you've got questions about starting an e-commerce business, consider the following tips and recommendations, along with some useful links and resources that can help.

Decide what you want to do and define your niche

Knowing what you are going to sell, how, and to whom is a critical part of your business plan: You really want to be 'specific' enough to get the right kind of customers and the least possible competition.

Start by first finding a niche in something you enjoy reading about or taking part in . . . The next thing you want to do is decide whether or not you are going to sell the products or be an affiliate of them.

If you need help finding your niche or deciding what to sell, these blog posts can help:

6 Tips for Finding a Business Idea and Turning it into an Entrepreneurial Reality (http://tinyurl.com/mvxws3k)

5 Ways to Find the Right Niche and Target Market for Your Small Business (http://tinyurl.com/mep9n47)

Have a plan

Starting any kind of business requires a documented plan. Without one, you'll lack focus, overspend, and struggle to deal with the curveballs that starting and running a business throws.

This blog post offers tips on writing a business plan: How a Simple Business Plan can Get you from A to Z, and Navigate all Things In-Between. (http://tinyurl.com/mt86gk3)

Build a Web site

A major factor in your success will be the creation of a Web site. Not all sites are created equal. You can spend a lot of money on a Web site. It may look pretty and busy but may not help you sell your product

For low-cost tips, read the section on How to Start a Website for Free.

Drive traffic to your site

Driving traffic to your site and increasing search engine optimization (SEO) is essential and one of the trickiest aspects of doing business online.

Technically, you have over three million potential customers (at any given time) that are going (past) your online store. They are not aware of you unless you start doing some form of promotion.

Start reading up on the various ways to achieve a higher search engine result . . . If you have the cash for it, you can always hire one of the numerous SEO firms to help you.

For tips on driving traffic to your site, read: Starting and Growing an Online Business: *An Entrepreneur's Checklist – How to use online and offline channels to market your site* (http://tinyurl.com/ks2o6qu)

The History of E-commerce
by Dave Roos - from How Stuff Works – reprinted by permission

Rather than do the research myself, I got permission to reproduce this great article that pretty much sums up what happened to make the world of e-commerce what it is today.

If you've been involved with the web for more than a dozen years, you'll get a kick out of the trip down memory lane that started it all.

Over the past 12 years, the Internet has changed the way we buy and sell goods and services. Do you remember buying airline tickets before the Internet? Can you imagine buying a new computer or car without doing hours of Web research? And Christmas shopping? You actually had to step foot in the mall...ugh.

By definition, e-commerce means the buying or selling of goods and services over the Internet. According to the Pew Internet & American Life Project, 66 percent of the adults online have purchased something over the Internet, whether it's books, shoes or a Caribbean cruise.

But if you extend e-commerce's definition to include researching products and services online without buying anything, or bidding on an online auction but not winning, then the number of adults who participate in e-commerce jumps to 93 percent [source: Pew Internet & American Life Project]. That's just about all of us.

Even with a slumping global economy, online retail sales continue to rise. According to recent forecasts by Forrester Research, online retail sales will increase 17 percent in 2008 to reach an annual total of $204 billion, with the biggest sellers being clothing, computers and cars [source: InformationWeek].

E-commerce's history is short but fascinating. Over the course of a few decades, networking and computing technology have improved at exponential rates. Powerful personal computers linked to global information networks have powered a whole new world of intellectual, social and financial interactions.

And this is only the beginning.

How did e-commerce get started? What were the first companies to really capitalize on the selling power of the Web? Read on to find out.

How E-commerce started

As far back as the 1960s, businesses were using primitive computer networks to conduct electronic transactions [source:123EDI]. Using something called Electronic Data Interchange (EDI), a company's computer system could share business documents -- invoices, order forms, shipping confirmation -- with another company's computer. In the beginning, each company had its own standards for formatting these documents. But in 1979, the American National Standards Institute (ANSI) came up with something called ASC X12, a universal standard for sharing business documents over electronic networks.

Prior to that, in the late 1960s, the military developed ARPAnet to ensure that crucial communications were circulated in the event of a nuclear attack. The original ARPAnet connected four large U.S. research universities and relied on huge, unwieldy computers. In 1971, researchers developed the Terminal Interface Processor (TIP) for dialing into the ARPAnet from an individual computer terminal [source: ARPAnet]. But the greatest networking evolution came in 1982, when ARPAnet switched over to Transmission Control Protocol and Internet Protocol (TCP/IP), the same packet-switched technology that powers the modern Internet.

By the early 1980s, individual computer users -- still mostly at major research universities -- were sending e-mails, participating in listservs and newsgroups, and sharing documents over networks like BITNET and USENET.

CompuServe was one of the first popular networking services for home PC users, providing tools like e-mail, message boards and chat rooms. In the mid-1980s, Compuserve added a service called the Electronic Mall, where users could purchase items directly from 110 online merchants [source: SmartComputing]. While the Electronic Mall wasn't a huge success, it was one of the first examples of e-commerce as we know it today.

In 1990, a researcher named Tim Berners-Lee at the European Organization for Nuclear Research (CERN, from its French name) proposed a hypertext-based web of information that a user could navigate using a simple interface called a browser. He called it the "WorldWideWeb" [source: NetValley]. And in 1991, the National Science Foundation lifted a ban on commercial businesses operating over the Internet, paving the way for Web-based e-commerce.

In 1993, Marc Andreesen at the National Center for Supercomputing Applications (NCSA) introduced the first widely distributed Web browser called Mosaic. Netscape 1.0's release in 1994 included an important security protocol called Secure Socket Layer (SSL) that encrypted messages on both the sending and receiving side of an online transaction. SSL ensured that personal information like names, addresses and credit card numbers could be encrypted as they passed over the Internet.

In 1994 and 1995, the first third-party services for processing online credit card sales began to appear [source: Keith Lamond]. First Virtual and CyberCash were two of the most popular. Also in 1995, a company called Verisign began developing digital IDs, or certificates, that verified the identity of online businesses. Soon, Verisign switched its focus to certifying that a Web site's e-commerce servers were properly encrypted and secure.

Now let's take a closer look at the two companies that transformed e-commerce in the mid-1990s: Amazon and eBay.

The Founding Fathers of E-commerce

In July 1995, Jeff Bezos boxed up the first book ever sold on Amazon.com from his Seattle garage [source: Amazon.com]. Within its first 30 days of business, the self-proclaimed "Earth's largest bookstore" sold books to online shoppers in all 50 U.S. states and 45 countries [source: Amazon.com].

With Amazon, Bezos tapped into a powerful new e-commerce market. Books, he had realized, were cheap to ship and easy to order directly from publishers. Publishers had already created vast digital archives of their titles on CD-ROM, something that could be uploaded to a Web site [source: Time].

Amazon.com set the standard for a customer-oriented e-commerce Web site. Users could search available titles by keyword, author or subject. They could browse books by category and even get personalized recommendations. They could also purchase books quickly and securely with the patented "one-click" checkout system.

But the most popular Amazon.com feature has always been the reader review option [source: E-commerce Land]. On Amazon, any registered member can write and publish a book review. And other users can rank each review, creating a hierarchy of top Amazon reviewers. Amazon's online community feel -- in addition to the steep discounts on many books -- has contributed to the site's popularity.

Amazon went public in 1997, and as the dot-com boom reached its pinnacle in 1999, Bezos was named Time's "Person of the Year." Amazon has expanded its offerings beyond books. It currently offers music, movies, electronics, toys, home and garden equipment, clothing, jewelry, video games and digital downloads. Amazon runs seven different international Web sites, has distribution and customer service centers in seven countries and employs more than 17,000 people worldwide. Yet despite its growth, Amazon hasn't always been a financial powerhouse: It didn't post its first quarterly profit until 2001 and its first annual profit until 2004 [source: Seattlepi.com]. But in the first quarter of 2008, Amazon announced a profit increase of 33 percent over last year, an impressive achievement in tough economic times [source:Associated Press].

Back in 1995, when Bezos was shipping books from his garage, Pierre Omidyar, a software programmer, started coding a simple Web site he called AuctionWeb. Omidyar was curious if people would use the Internet to bid on each other's used items. Looking around for something to sell, Omidyar picked up a broken laser pointer. Within a day, it had sold for $14.83 [source: eBay]. Omidyar e-mailed the buyer to make sure the guy knew it was broken. The buyer's response? "I'm a collector of broken laser pointers" [source: eBay]. Welcome to eBay.

eBay leveled the e-commerce playing field. You didn't have to be a Web entrepreneur or an existing business to sell things online. All you had to do was raid your attic, post a listing, and there was a good chance that someone, somewhere, would pay money for your old junk. In 1996, with two full-time employees, eBay sold $7.2 million worth of goods. By 1997, with the help of a Beanie Babies frenzy, eBay sold $95 million in goods. In 2007, eBay sold $52.5 billion in auctions, had more than 220 million registered users and 13,000 employees [source: eBay].

Both eBay and Amazon paved the way for today's e-commerce merchant. Consumers can buy almost anything online, including shoes, home goods and even a real shark's tooth. Just type "unusual items for sale" in a search engine, and see what comes up.

So What is E-commerce - really?

Electronic commerce, commonly known as E-commerce is a type of industry where the buying and selling of products or services is conducted over electronic systems such as the Internet, Web and other computer networks.

Electronic commerce draws on technologies such as mobile commerce, electronic funds transfer, supply chain management, Internet marketing, online transaction processing, electronic data interchange (EDI), inventory management systems, and automated data collection systems.

Modern electronic commerce typically uses the World Wide Web at least at one point in the transaction's life-cycle, although it may encompass a wider range of technologies such as e-mail, mobile devices, social media, and telephones as well.

Electronic commerce is generally considered to be the sales aspect of e-business.

It also consists of the exchange of data to facilitate the financing and payment aspects of business transactions.

It is a market entry strategy where the company may or may not have a physical presence.

In the world of marketing there are two primary philosophies:

1. Get somebody to place an order now and

2. Generate a targeted mailing list so that future sales can be made as a result of the list.

As a result of these two primary objectives, E-commerce can be divided into 6 subsections:

1. E-tailing or "virtual storefront" on web sites with online catalogs, sometimes gathered into a "virtual mall"
2. Buying or selling on your own web sites and/or online marketplaces
3. The gathering and use of demographic data through web contacts and social media

4. Electronic data interchange, the business-to-business exchange of data
5. E-mail used as media for reaching prospective and established customers (for example, with newsletters)
6. Business-to-business buying and selling.

All of these sections are designed to increase the profitability of your business enterprise but there is no standard formula for improving profitability; it depends entirely on specific circumstances and the relative strengths and weaknesses of your business.

In other words, any profit improvement strategy must focus on either or both of two things:

1. Sell it for more money or
2. Reduce the cost to provide it.

There's an old adage*:*

"It's not what you make, it's what you keep".

Don't forget that when you sell something, either goods or services, you have two basic costs – the product/service costs themselves and the overhead or cost of doing business.

In addition to providing an unprecedented time-to-market presence for both new and existing business enterprises, e-commerce has become invaluable in reducing the costs of doing business by saving time in delivering everything from basic advertising information to the electronic delivery of digital goods.
Properly implemented into your overall business strategy, e-commerce can become the most powerful tool you have to make sure that your enterprise is profitable.

Overview of E-Commerce

There is a formal definition of e-commerce that reads something like this: *E-commerce is replacing face to face business relationships with the tools of technology.*

For all practical purposes, most people would say that e-commerce is buying something from a Web site using a credit card for payment.

You can offer your physical products for sale from your Web site, collect payments, and then ship them.

Practically speaking, it's like the mail order business on steroids because what we've done is replace the old paper order processing systems with e-mail and online order forms.

What we're talking about with successful e-commerce is **Internet Marketing!**

To understand whether Internet marketing has all of the opportunities it claims to have, you first need to understand what the concept is all about so let's start with the basics.

What is Internet Marketing?

In a very broad sense, any method that helps you make money from the Internet by publicizing a product or service for sale is Internet marketing.

For example, if you have an e-book and you sell it on the Internet to make money, then what you are doing is Internet marketing.

It's not necessary that the product be exclusively yours and there are a variety of ways in which you can acquire products from others like:

- Getting reseller rights to products is one way in which you do this.
- Becoming an affiliate for some Web site that is selling a product is another way to do this.

In these examples, you're not selling your own product, but you are publicizing it on the Internet all the same, which is why it fits within the definition of Internet marketing.

Consequently, affiliate marketing is a subset of Internet marketing.

Of course, you'll be more comfortable if you follow the mantra of *sell what you know* and only sell what you believe in! In other words, they should be things that you feel confident selling to other people.

Here are five great sources for e-commerce products that you can sell on your e-commerce Web site and feel confident in providing them to your customer.

1. ***Thrift Stores, Flea Markets, and Garage Sales***

Start your own thrift store online!

You can sell any number of used items including pre-owned clothing, collectibles, house wares, toys and more in your e-commerce store.

2. ***Affiliate Programs***

You can find an affiliate program for any product you wish to sell in your e-commerce store.

Amazon.com is especially useful as you can use product pictures easily within your own shopping cart system.

Just provide a link to the retailer and pocket your affiliate commission.

3. ***Drop Shippers***

Drop shipping is a method of getting products to your customers with minimal involvement from you.

The distributor warehouses the inventory and takes care of shipping. All you have to do is take orders and then tell the drop shipper to ship the product to your customer.

Drop shipping is a very popular and simple method of getting started in e-commerce.

4. Bulk Wholesale

With a resale certificate, any person or business can get involved with bulk wholesale purchasing.

You can buy a bulk load: case, pallet, or truck load, or whatever product you would like to sell.

Following the receipt of an order through your e-commerce store, you will have to ship the order yourself.

Running an e-commerce Web site using bulk wholesale goods is riskier than the other methods as there is always the chance that you will be stuck with merchandise that will not sell.

5. Handcrafted Items

Many local hobbyists and crafts people would love to make money with their handcrafted items.

An e-commerce store is an excellent way of selling these handcrafted items.

No matter what you make or broker for someone else like jewelry, needlework, clothing, pottery, or paintings, you can sell it through an e-commerce Web site.

How do you profit with E-Commerce?

There are eight primary methods for making a profit with e-commerce:

1. Profits on sales
2. Commissions on sales
3. Referral fees
4. Subscription fees
5. Advertising/sponsorship fees
6. Cost reductions by delivering digital goods instead of physical goods
7. Cost reductions in advertising and promotion
8. Rapid reordering and aftermarket sales through digital notifications

We've included the following quick overview of each of these elements and how e-commerce can positively enhance their profitability:

1. **Profits on sales –** This is the basic sales tenant; buy low, sell high.
2. **Commissions on sales –** you sell their stuff and get a percentage of the sale
3. **Referral fees –** you refer to business to someone else and they pay you a referral fee for the sales lead
4. **Subscription fees –** You sell information and get paid for it on a regular basis
5. **Advertising/sponsorship fees –** you let someone else place advertisements on your web site and they pay you a fee for the rental of the space
6. **Cost reductions by delivering digital goods instead of physical goods** – This are things like e-books and other materials that can be converted to digital form and delivered without production, inventory or shipping costs.
7. **Cost reductions in advertising and promotion** – Using low cost/no cost electronic advertising to get business as opposed to paying for the printing and postage of conventional advertising
8. **Rapid reordering and aftermarket sales through digital notifications** - using a concept called 'drip marketing' to constantly remind existing customers of new products and services that are related to their prior purchase –also known as the aftermarket or accessory market.

E-commerce is primarily about marketing

For most of the people who are considering e-commerce as a revenue source, marketing is the primary usage that will be employed.

In order to be successful in any kind of marketing efforts, including e-commerce efforts, your offering must be appropriate.

Webster's loosely defines "appropriate" as correct and proper so the question really becomes:

- Appropriate for whom?
- Appropriate for what products or services?
- Appropriate for what market?
- Appropriate for whose budget (including yours)?

Appropriate is NOT about right VS wrong, good VS bad, expensive VS cheap, or doing what someone else is doing to be successful in their marketing efforts. It's exclusively about what is correct and proper for your success based on the realities of the time, money, experience, and goals of your organization.

What's appropriate for a Fortune 500 company do be doing is probably inappropriate for your organization.

It might not be, but just because someone else is doing something that is making them successful does NOT mean that it will work the same way for you.

Conscientiously evaluate your marketing efforts and make sure they are consistent with your overall goals, objectives, and budgets so that the results reflect your goals and not someone else's before you decide that e-commerce is going to be the answer to all your needs.

The fundamentals of marketing

Before we get into the specifics of e-commerce marketing, it's important to understand that from a practical standpoint, marketing is truly the project management used to create the master plan and incorporates the following seven elements involved with getting and keeping clients.

Here's a simplified overview of what actually makes of a marketing program so that you'll have an understanding of what they are and how to use them effectively in your own e-commerce marketing programs.

1. Market research – Finding out what goods and/or services your targeted base really wants and is willing to pay for.
2. Product researches – Figuring out what goods and/or services best fit the clients defined needs and are willing to pay for.
3. Advertising – Creating the awareness that your goods and/or services exist.
4. Sales – Getting the client to pay you for your goods and/or services.
5. Fulfillment – The delivery of your goods and/or services.
6. Customer service – Rectifying any inequities in the delivery of your goods and/or services or supplying services such as repair and/or instructions as a part of the program.
7. Aftermarket sales – Selling the client additional goods and/or services as an adjunct to the initial sale. The two parts of marketing

The three types of marketing

There are three kinds of Marketing: Indirect, Quasi-Direct, and Direct

This particular axiom refers to a combination of the advertising and distribution elements of the marketing process.

It needs to be addressed because the different types of marketing and involve a different kind of mindset on both a part of the marketer and the customer.

Let's describe the three kinds of marketing so that you understand the differences between them:

#1 - Indirect marketing - this is the kind of marketing effort that we experience every day when we deal with a retail store.

The supplier of goods or services markets to a distribution network that eventually markets to a retail outlet that ultimately retails to the consumer.

The overall process is indirect from the supplier to the end user and different levels of marketing and advertising are used to get the merchandise from the top of the bottom of the chain.

Because each level within the indirect marketing chain has different pricing, distribution, advertising, and customer concerns, each element of the indirect marketing process is definitively different and to try and use one method at another level usually result in economic disaster.

Simply defined, this means that in order to be successful in an indirect marketing program, each level must be addressed independently and to the results examined carefully so that changes can be made that keep the pipeline flowing smoothly.

#2 – Quasi-Direct marketing-this is also known as multilevel marketing. What makes this particular type of marketing distinctive is that the efforts are a combination of dealer and distributor promotion targeted towards the end user with a touch of the carnival huckster thrown in for good measure.

Multilevel organizations promote the fact that they jump over several levels of middle distribution and can therefore save you a great deal of money because you are purchasing closer to factory direct.

This creates the need for the advertising and promotion in this area to explain the multiple levels of costing and distribution in order to show how their program actually circumvents these steps and offers the end user the same quality and performance but at a lesser cost because all of the middlemen have been eliminated.

This does not negate the need to extol the virtues of the products and services but it does create the need to explain why it is more beneficial and advantageous to do business in this manner than it is to be a retail customer.

#3 Direct marketing - Direct marketing is defined as the process whereby the supplier advertises and promotes directly to the end user, the end user responds directly to the supplier, and the supplier ships or fulfills directly to the end user with no middle persons or distribution network in between.

Most people are familiar with this process from the world of direct mail marketing where the supplier mails out an advertising piece and we respond directly to them in they, in turn, ship directly back to us.

Direct mail is actually a part of the direct response marketing industry and includes not only direct mail, but includes magazine advertising, newspaper advertising, catalog advertising, television advertising, radio advertising, billboards, bus bench advertising, and of course the Internet.

All these mediums allow the supplier to directly solicit business from the end user and the end user to respond directly to the supplier.

When you are engaging in direct response marketing, you must think like the consumer and look to their specific wants and needs with respect to what it is that you're offering.

This is the most blatant or *in-your-face* type of marketing because the results, be they positive or negative, will be directly traceable to your specific efforts because there is no additional distribution, advertising, or promotional staff in between to dilute or diversify the effects of your specific advertising efforts.

Direct response marketers have become extremely successful because they have the ability to directly monitor and modify the advertising and promotion that they exert and take immediate corrective action without having to worry about multiple levels of dealers or distribution.

Although e-commerce is being successfully utilized in all three types of marketing, most of the people who are embarking on an e-commerce enterprise are planning on using a direct marketing approach so that's what we'll concentrate on in this manual.

The two parts of direct marketing and where e-commerce fits in

Although you've probably noted that e-commerce works well for all seven of the elements of marketing, its numbers 3, 4, and 5, or advertising, sales, and fulfillment where it really shines.

Actually, that's kind of a half-truth because e-commerce doesn't work as well for advertising as most people would have you think.

Advertising is creating the awareness that something exists and its only purpose, for our application, is to generate sales.

Successful marketers have long known that finding the right place to put advertising so that it reaches the defined target customer base is key to its success, and a broad based vehicle, like the web with over a trillion pages of information, is too broad an advertising vehicle to be truly effective on its own.

In conventional sales, we have the *"pitch"* and the *"close"* where the pitch is defined as the advertising and the close is the actual sale.

This is referred to as "two-step" marketing and although it's been around for a long time, the electronic elements of e-commerce have streamlined the second step, the close, but not the first, the pitch.

Although the web can be used for the pitch, its broad base doesn't work well for initial advertising and needs the support of conventional advertising, or a referral network of already existing prospects, as a feed tube for our leads.

This is borne out by remembering that with over one trillion pages of information available, virtually no one is going to find your advertising by accident and since most people, no matter how good Google, Yahoo, and Bing gets, are non-proficient at doing effective searches on the web, so your e-commerce site is going to go unnoticed.

What successful e-commerce practitioners have found is that a combination of conventional advertising, especially to gather the initial contact information of prospective clients, coupled with the low cost, high speed, and convenience of the e-commerce tools, work the best.

Consider how many times in the past week you've seen an ad in movies, on TV, in magazines, newspapers, newsletters, billboards, busses, bus benches, the sides of truck, and on people's rear windows that lists their web site.

This is done because these locations are appropriate places to get the attention of prospective clients without depending on them to stumble across their web sites.

What has been proven to work best is to utilize conventional advertising methodologies, coupled with referral network, to create the initial contact with your prospective client and then use the tools of e-commerce to maintain contact and purse the sales aspect of the transaction.

For example, if you already have a mailing list of past clients or prospective clients, you might start by mailing them a postcard announcing that you are now offering your goods and services on your web site.

The sheer expediency of reviewing and ordering from the convenience of their computer gives you an advantage in that they don't have to travel, put up with crowds and traffic, can pay for the purchase with their credit card, and can get the process completed without any grief and hassle makes this something of a perfect business model.

This is where e-commerce shines more brightly than anywhere else – the ability to compress time and remove the conventional hassles of doing business.

What is direct marketing?

Since e-commerce is primarily about direct marketing, it's a good idea to understand what direct marketing is all about.

Barron's Business Dictionary defines direct marketing as *selling via a promotion delivered individually to the prospective customer.*

Direct marketing differs from general marketing in that the result of a promotion is measurable in terms of response; also, direct marketing is largely dependent upon the use of customer files and lists.

Frequently associated with mail order firms, direct marketing also includes a variety of promotion media such as door-to-door selling, videotext services, newspaper inserts, telemarketing , take-one cards, and package inserts.

Direct marketing is a more personal type of promotion than advertising.

The primary users have been magazine publishers, catalog houses, political campaign organizations, and financial institutions.

According to the official definition of the Direct Marketing Association (DMA), direct marketing is an *"interactive system of marketing which uses one or more advertising media to affect a measurable response and/or transaction at any location."*

While there are many other possible definitions, the DMA captures the four basic concepts that set direct marketing apart from traditional marketing.

The notion of interactivity, or one-to-one communication between the marketer and the prospect or customer, is one factor that distinguishes direct marketing from general advertising and other types of marketing.

Direct marketing makes an offer and asks for a response.

By developing a history of offers and responses, direct marketers acquire knowledge of their prospects and customers, resulting in more effective targeting. Measurability also sets direct marketing apart from general advertising and other forms of marketing.

Direct marketers can measure the response to any offer. Measurability allows direct marketers to test a variety of lists, offers, media—virtually any aspect of a campaign—in order to allocate marketing resources to the most effective combination of elements.

Direct marketing uses a variety of media, including mail, magazine ads, newspaper ads, television and radio spots, infomercials (also television but longer format), free standing inserts (FSIs), and card decks.

This flexibility allows direct marketing to provide interactivity and measurability and still take advantage of new technologies.

By being adaptable to virtually any media, direct marketing will lead marketers into the twenty-first century as interactive television, the information superhighway, and other new technologies become a reality. (Note that this definition, although basically sound, was formulated in the late 1980's)

Finally, in direct marketing, the transaction may take place at any location and is not limited to retail stores or fixed places of business.

The transaction may take place in the consumer's home or office via mail, over the phone, on the Internet, or through interactive television. It may also occur away from the home or office, as at a kiosk, for example.

It is necessary to distinguish direct marketing from direct mail or mail-order businesses, although direct marketing encompasses those two concepts.

Direct mail is an advertising medium, one of several media that direct marketers utilize. Mail order is a distribution channel, as are retail outlets and personal selling.

E-commerce fills dual roles by offering the ability to advertise as well as being a vehicle for the actual sales process and a delivery vehicle for virtual products.

7

The seven types of e-commerce business – and why it's essential to know which type you are

The type of e-commerce business you are in affects everything you do with that business.

If you have physical stores then you need to keep a certain amount of stock on the shelves – or your store will look empty – at the same time keep your web site in stock too.

For example there are those that sell just one thing. Likewise, if you have a storefront site, you'll need to keep it stocked with new products as well.

Then there are others, like Amazon, who sells almost everything!

Some have stores, some sell on eBay, others send out catalogues.

If you sell on eBay you don't have to spend too much time on your marketing – eBay brings you traffic, you don't have to, but you do need to streamline your processes as much as possible to reduce your overhead costs.

There is an easy way to classify e-commerce businesses that splits them into just seven different types.

Understanding which of these your e-commerce business fits into will fundamentally change the way you run and market your business.

The seven types of e-commerce business explained

1. **Online Only** - the only way to see the products is online E.G. www.beyondtherack.com; www.NoMoreRack.com

2. **Mail Order** - a transactional web site plus a printed catalogue, and possibly one or two physical stores E.G. www.Grunt.com; www.tigerdirect.com

3. **Big Bricks and Clicks** - These are chains that have lots of physical stores and an e-commerce web site E.G.: www.target.com; www.Bestbuy.com; www.staples.com.

4. **Boutique Bricks and Clicks** - just one or two physical locations plus the e-commerce web site E.G. www.Roundsmiller.com; www.Clutterology.com

5. **Mainstream Piggyback -** using sites like Amazon or eBay to market the products, with no web site of their own E.G. – http://www.ebay.ca/usr/jojoandyou

6. **Niche Piggyback** - where sellers of similar products come together to market more easily, usually retains their own blog or e-commerce site elsewhere too. http://www.rainforest-alliance.org

7. **Full Multichannel -** Using multiple stores, catalogues, and e-commerce – by far the most complex and most difficult to achieve and run. E.G - http://www.sears.com/

Although e-commerce and affiliate marketing (which is explained in detail later on) has been dubbed *Mail Order on Steroids,* mail order is very different from online only because a catalogue exists for a long time which puts restrictions on your merchandising – you've got to keep products in stock for longer, and you are very likely to have to deal with backorders.

Bricks and Clicks are different to other types because you've got all the overheads of stores to deal with. They also have the opportunity to use those stores to drive traffic to their web sites – and can create a pick-up-in-store delivery option.

The Piggyback types are a whole new way to do business online – no more struggling to get your web site right, just use someone else's and let them bring you business.

Then there's Full Multichannel – encompassing it all, and the most heavily reliant on good integrated systems.

How do I work out which I am?

That's fairly straight forward – it's all to do with where you sell your products.

- If you sell from a physical store then you're either Full Multichannel, or one of the Bricks and Clicks types.
- If you have a catalogue you're either Full Multichannel or Mail Order.
- If you don't have an e-commerce web site of your own then you're one of the Piggyback types.

Affiliate Marketing Explained

Affiliate marketing is a type of performance-based marketing in which a business rewards one or more affiliates for each visitor or customer brought by the affiliate's own marketing efforts.

The industry has four core players: the merchant (also known as retailer or brand), the network (that contains offers for the affiliate to choose from and also takes care of the payments), the publisher (also known as the affiliate), and the customer.

Affiliate marketing is commonly confused with referral marketing, as both forms of marketing use third parties to drive sales to the retailer.

However, affiliate and referral are distinct forms of marketing and the main difference between them is that affiliate marketing relies purely on financial motivations to drive sales while referral marketing relies on trust and personal relationships to drive sales.

Affiliate marketing, and its associated income, can be divided into three primary categories:

Unattached, Related, and involved, which relates to how you are associated with the product or products that you may be an affiliate for.

Unattached Affiliate Marketing

These are your basic Pay-Per-Click (PPC) affiliate marketing campaigns where you have no presence and no authority in the niche of the product you're promoting.

There's no connection between you and the end consumer, and all you're doing is showing an affiliate link in front of someone's face via Google Adwords, Facebook ads or whatever, in hopes that they'll click on your link, buy the product, and you'll earn a commission.

The reason why this type of affiliate marketing is so attractive is because no presence or authority in a niche is needed!

It takes time to build up a reputation and trust with certain groups of people online, and many people are just too scared to commit to working on a blog or web site, or just don't have the time. For many, this is their only option.

This is an income generating technique but NOT a business model where you can build relationships with the end user.

With PPC affiliate marketing, you become a behind the scenes middle man.

Related Affiliate Marketing

Another form of affiliate marketing is Related Affiliate Marketing.

This is where you have some sort of presence online, whether it's through a blog, a podcast, videos, or whatever – and you have affiliate links to products related to your niche, but they're for products you don't actually use.

Placing affiliate links on your site that are related to your niche is a great strategy to earn an extra income.

Whether it's in the sidebar in banner form, or in a text link at the bottom of your blog post, because you have a web site and some authority, people will trust you and your decision to place the ad on your site.

Related Affiliate Marketing is great, but statistics show that 95 percent of affiliate marketing revenue comes from involved affiliate marketing.

Involved Affiliate Marketing

Involved Affiliate Marketing is where you've used a product or service, truly believe in it, and personally recommend it to your audience.

Not in a banner ad or somewhere that says "recommended resources", but within your content, as part of your life and your strategy for whatever it is you're talking about.

The product almost becomes something people "have to have", because it's part of the process.

It's your involvement and experience with the product that makes that offer so attractive.

There is, however, a level of responsibility that you have to uphold while making these kinds of recommendations, especially if you have a lot of authority and influence over your followers.

This is the complete opposite of PPC, where you're not even seen by the consumer in order for the transaction to take place. Instead, this is you talking directly to those who may need a product that you're offering, who have their ears and eyes on you.

This is not using your money in order to make money, like with PPC. It's using your reputation, trust and authority in order to get others to take your recommendation, use it, and pay you something in return in the form of a commission.

Using Drop Shipping in E-Commerce

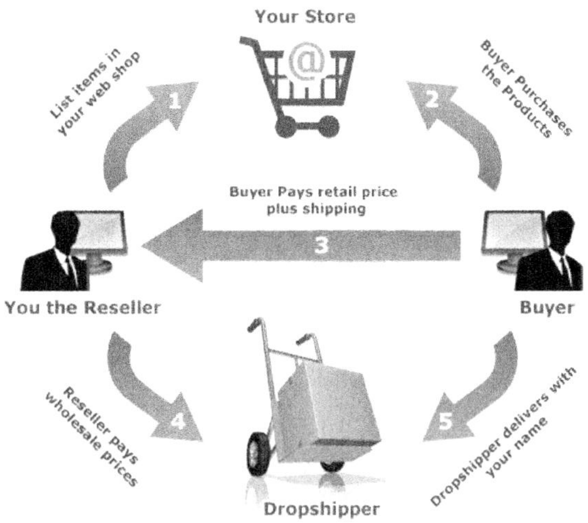

Drop shipping is an order fulfillment strategy where the retailer does not keep product in inventory, but relies on wholesalers or manufacturers to actually ship orders to customers.

This arrangement has several advantages that make it attractive to online merchants.

When a customer places an order for a drop shipped product online, the retailer receives the order and payment for the order, and then either automatically or manually contacts the wholesaler or manufacturer, issuing a purchase order for the item and providing instructions for shipping directly to the customer. The wholesaler or manufacturer ships the product, and the retailer earns a profit.

There are at least five good reasons that almost any e-commerce retailer should consider drop shipping.

1. A Broad Product Offering

Drop shipping allows merchants to offer many more products for sale than what might be feasible if that merchant had to inventory everything.

Imagine a retailer who sells specialty coffee and tea both online and in a boutique. The physical store might have limited space for storing espresso machines, so that the retailer may only offer one or two models in store.

But online, if the retailer has drop shipping arrangements in place with several espresso machine makers, that retailer might offer dozens of different options.

Having a broad range of options can also help marketing, since each product page can be a landing page, entry in a comparison-shipping engine, or additional page for Google or Bing to index.

These additional products are a way of introducing a greater number of potential customers to the store.

2. Come to Market More Quickly

While it takes just as long to post a drop shipped product to an e-commerce platform as it does a product that is in inventory, drop shipping may help a merchant come to market more quickly.

Drop shipping eliminates waiting times when products are shipped from the distributor or manufacturer to the merchant. In some cases, this can be a few weeks. With drop shipping, a merchant can start selling the moment the product is published on the e-commerce site.

3. Explore New Lines

Drop shipping gives merchants a way to test new products without having to bring in inventory.

For example, imagine a retailer that sells tack (saddles, bridles, and other equine-related products) for what is called “Western” style riding. Occasionally, this online retailer gets requests for “English” style saddles or riding apparel. A drop shipping agreement with a supplier of “English” gear would allow the retailer to explore how well those products would sell, without committing hard dollars.

An underlying theme in points one to three has been that merchants employing a drop shipping strategy don’t have to keep products in inventory.

Quite simply, since drop-shipping agreements generally do not require any upfront investment, a retailer can significantly reduce its investment in products.

This also means that some e-commerce start-ups don’t need as much money as one might think to get up and selling.

4. More Time

In a drop shipping arrangement, the retailer does not receive, stack, store, pull, pack, or ship products. All of these tasks are time consuming, which means drop shipping saves time.

In a startup e-commerce business where the storeowner may also be the box packer, this additional time will be available to actually sell products, which should benefit the company.

In larger operations, the time savings may result in a reduction, or stabilizing, of labor costs.

The Downside of Drop Shipping

Drop shipping does have its downside. For example, it creates customer service challenges as orders can get mixed up, inventory levels change, and product returns become complicated.

Profit margins for drop shipped items are often razor thin too. For example, some manufacturers charge an additional $10 per item drop ship fee on top of the item's cost and any shipping charges.

If a brand's products sells for about $59.99, with a cost of around $30, a product sold from inventory has about $29.99 in margin while a product sold via drop shipping is at $19.99.

If a retailer offers free shipping on orders above $50, an additional $5 to $10 of profit is also gone. Add an average return rate, payment card fees, and the cost of pay-per-click advertising, and there may not be a lot left.

With these potential challenges, drop shipping may work best in conjunction with inventorying some products.

Resources for drop shipping:

www.worldwidebrands.com/wwb/ordernow_p1.asp

The World's Largest Directory of Drop Shippers and Bulk Distributors is now open to small home-based online sellers!

Find out exactly who the Top-Level Certified Wholesalers are for the products you want to sell on Amazon, eBay and in your Online Store. Updated weekly with new Certified Wholesalers we are the ONLY wholesale directory you'll ever need.

Instant Access - Full Membership................ $299

Free List of Dropshipping Suppliers
http://www.watchmanadvisors.com/list-of-dropshipping-suppliers

Pay Per Click

Pay Per Click (PPC) (also called cost per click) is an internet advertising model used to direct traffic to web sites, in which advertisers pay the publisher (typically a web site owner) when the ad is clicked.

It is defined simply as *"the amount spent to get an advertisement clicked."*

With search engines, advertisers typically bid on keyword phrases relevant to their target market. Content sites commonly charge a fixed price per click rather than use a bidding system. PPC display advertisements, also known as "banner" ads, are shown on web sites or search engine results with related content that have agreed to show ads.

In contrast to the generalized portal, which seeks to drive a high volume of traffic to one site, PPC implements the so-called affiliate model, which provides purchase opportunities wherever people may be surfing.

It does this by offering financial incentives (in the form of a percentage of revenue) to affiliated partner sites.

The affiliates provide purchase-point click through to the merchant. It is a pay-for-performance model: if an affiliate does not generate sales, it represents no cost to the merchant.

Variations include banner exchange, pay-per-click, and revenue sharing programs.

Websites that utilize PPC ads will display an advertisement when a keyword query matches an advertiser's keyword list, or when a content site displays relevant content.

Such advertisements are called sponsored links or sponsored ads, and appear adjacent to, above, or beneath organic results on search engine results pages, or anywhere a web developer chooses on a content site.

Purpose

Pay-Per-Click, along with cost per impression and cost per order, are used to assess the cost effectiveness and profitability of internet marketing. Pay-Per-Click has an advantage over cost per impression in that it tells us something about how effective the advertising was.

Clicks are a way to measure attention and interest. Inexpensive ads that few people click on will have a low cost per impression and a high Pay-Per-Click. If the main purpose of an ad is to generate a click, then Pay-Per-Click is the preferred metric.

Once a certain number of web impressions are achieved, the quality and placement of the advertisement will affect click through rates and the resulting pay-per-click.

Construction

Pay-Per-Click is calculated by dividing the advertising cost by the number of clicks generated by an advertisement. The basic formula is:

Pay-per-click ($) = Advertising cost ($) ÷ Ads clicked (#)[1]

There are two primary models for determining pay-per-click: flat-rate and bid-based. In both cases, the advertiser must consider the potential value of a click from a given source.

This value is based on the type of individual the advertiser is expecting to receive as a visitor to his or her web site, and what the advertiser can gain from that visit, usually revenue, both in the short term as well as in the long term.

As with other forms of advertising targeting is key, and factors that often play into PPC campaigns include the target's interest (often defined by a search term they have entered into a search engine, or the content of a page that they are browsing), intent (e.g., to purchase or not), location (for geo targeting), and the day and time that they are browsing.

Flat-rate PPC

In the flat-rate model, the advertiser and publisher agree upon a fixed amount that will be paid for each click.

In many cases the publisher has a rate card that lists the Pay-Per-Click (PPC) within different areas of their web site or network.

These various amounts are often related to the content on pages, with content that generally attracts more valuable visitors having a higher PPC than content that attracts less valuable visitors.

However, in many cases advertisers can negotiate lower rates, especially when committing to a long-term or high-value contract.
The flat-rate model is particularly common to comparison shopping engines, which typically publish rate cards. However, these rates are sometimes minimal, and advertisers can pay more for greater visibility.

These sites are usually neatly compartmentalized into product or service categories, allowing a high degree of targeting by advertisers. In many cases, the entire core content of these sites is paid ads.

Bid-based PPC

The advertiser signs a contract that allows them to compete against other advertisers in a private auction hosted by a publisher or, more commonly, an advertising network.

Each advertiser informs the host of the maximum amount that he or she is willing to pay for a given ad spot (often based on a keyword), usually using online tools to do so. The auction plays out in an automated fashion every time a visitor triggers the ad spot.

When the ad spot is part of a search engine results page (SERP), the automated auction takes place whenever a search for the keyword that is being bid upon occurs.

All bids for the keyword that target the searcher's geo-location, the day and time of the search, etc. are then compared and the winner determined.

Membership Sites

Membership sites, or sub-sites of your primary web site, are sites with specific areas for members.

Generally members pay some type of fee to join the site. It could be a monthly, annually, or lifetime free.

The main advantage for the affiliate is the recurring income from the site.

The more recently refined definition says that defined Membership Sites are a "*community of like-minded people that focus on a cause or topic that they believed in.*"

To access this information, your customers will pay you a monthly fee that will re-bill every month which means that having a Membership Site generates a passive income, which means having this kind of site is like getting the expected money you desired with very less effort required.

Membership Sites usually require that you pay for membership and the products are received for free, which means that Membership Sites are not about constantly selling something new to the people's list; instead it is one way of putting people in Membership Sites.

The reason that people will sign up is that they expect and anticipate receiving new contents about a topic that is of interest to them.

The advantages of having a membership site

There are many advantages to having a membership site if you're interested in making money.

Most people create products and only make money when the transaction takes place.

Membership sites are different in that they pay you a passive income whether anyone purchases anything new or not.

These are the 6 reasons why you should have a membership site.

1. **Consistent revenue with a gradual rise.** This is the big one. Instead of hoping your products keep on making sales and you keep on seeing a profit, a membership site will bring in consistent revenue with a gradual rise. Imagine charging $49 a month and having 200 members. That's $9800 every month! Products that don't have a membership do not bring in this consistent revenue as often.

2. **There is less work on your part after the first year.** During the first year of a membership site, you would have created the videos and content that went into the membership site. In future years, you will already have the product in place which will allow you to spend more time creating other membership sites and promoting the ones that you already have.

3. **Having a membership site is one of the seven traits of internet millionaires**. The membership site also does a good job at laying out 5 of the other traits as well. Imagine how your life would change if you were making over $1 million every year.

4. **Membership sites give you the option to promote your other products**. There are many people who give away free products just for joining the membership site. These people commonly give away their own books to all of their members. These people still get to make a profit, and being a bestselling author becomes a lot easier.

5. **You can build a community in the membership site's forum**. The first year is a challenging process because responding to other people in the forum may take up a lot of your time. However, the forum puts you as the #1 go-to expert, and the forum will eventually become a strong community. Then, members will be answering other member's questions. Everyone ends up winning!

6. **You gain credibility.** Imagine you met with two entrepreneurs. One entrepreneur says he has a lot of potential while the other says he has multiple membership sites and books. If you could only choose one, which entrepreneur would you choose to work with? Chances are you would choose the entrepreneur with multiple membership sites and books.

These are also the kinds of decisions that big media outlets make before interviewing people.

7 Tips for Creating and Running Your First Membership Site

#1: Start before you think you're ready

You'll never be completely ready. Start it anyway.

Try it: If you're not sure that you have enough to offer, you can:

Start off at a ridiculously low fee. Let your charter members know they'll basically be acting as guinea pigs — and that you'd love their feedback and ideas.

Aim for a minimum viable product (MVP) rather than perfection. Your membership site doesn't need to be the next Amazon.com.

#2: Learn from membership sites you belong to

Do you belong to any membership sites? Look at what others are profiting from like:

- Monthly seminars (sometimes with guest speakers)
- Monthly Q&A calls
- Member forums

Think about:

What's working well for you in that site? What makes it worth the monthly fee — and how could you replicate this?

What doesn't work for you? If you're struggling to find time to use the resources, for instance, how could the site owner make that easier?

Bring in other learning experiences here, too; perhaps you had a great course (or a terrible one) during college, and you can use aspects of that to help you with your planning.

#3: Interact and engage with members

Although some membership sites are simply dripped feeds of content, with little or no input from the owner, members will have a much stronger reason to join if they know they'll have insider access to you.

Depending on your set-up, that could mean:

- Live seminars or webinars where members can ask questions through chat or over the phone
- Forums where you post regularly, providing help and support for your members.
- A text chat room where you hold "office hours" or similar
- A private Facebook group where you chat with members

A contact form that ensures you spot members' messages quickly in your inbox

- Try it: Even if you're busy, stay involved with you membership site. It might help to:

Set aside time on a regular basis to interact. E.g. you might check forums daily, send out an email weekly, and hold a live webinar every three months.

Lead the way with interaction. (This is on my "get better at" list.) If your forums are quiet, start an extra topic or two — members may be shy about breaking the ice.

#4: Run group events and challenges

Maybe you've provided tons of great materials — e-courses in bite-sized chunks, pre-recorded seminars, video tutorials — but members just don't seem to be engaging with them.

Some people enjoy working at their own pace, alone, but many find it easier to stay motivated and on track when they're going through materials with a group.

You don't necessarily need to have a big event to get people involved — in fact, simple is probably better.

Try it: There's a wonderful buzz and energy in working as a group, but this can be tough to foster when members live in different countries and time zones.

You could aim to:

Have regular events, challenges, group courses, or similar. This might simply mean using existing materials in your membership site and going through them week by week.

Make it easy to participate ... and fun! Offering prizes creates a great incentive for members to get involved.

#5: Give out free places

One of the very best things you can do with your membership site is to let a handful of people in for free.

That might sound like a stupid idea — after all, that's money you could be missing out on. But if you give these free places to people who wouldn't have been able to join otherwise, you might gain some valuable credibility and feedback that you wouldn't have received otherwise..

If you have audience members who you'd love to have on board, but who probably won't be able to afford your fees, consider letting them in for free.

They might be people who regularly leave thoughtful comments on your blog, or tweet your posts, or even write about you on their site.

These lovely people are often your greatest fans — and they may well become some of the most committed, helpful members of your site.

If offering free places will eat into your margins too much, consider having discounted places for students/ under-18s/retirees.

#6: Help members find their way around as your site grows

When you start your membership site, your main concern will probably be ensuring that members know they're getting plenty of content for their money.

After a year or so, you'll realize that there's more than enough content — and your members need an easy route through the maze.

If, for instance, you put out one recorded seminar and one Q&A every month, and one course of video lessons every three months, you'll have twelve seminars, twelve Q&As and four courses after a year — plus any extras you might have created.

Make sure you have a "Welcome" page or similar for new members to help them get started quickly. Update this on a regular basis.

Remind members of older resources they might have missed. If you produce a new seminar or course, link to older ones that are relevant.

#7: Shift and adapt based on members' needs

Today's world is dynamic, not static and your membership site won't always look the same. Over time, you might find that what sounded like a great idea six months ago simply isn't working any more.

Keep an eye on member engagement and involvement, and don't doggedly pursue things that no-one seems to care much about — however awesome you think they are!

That might mean switching from live webinars to recorded ones (or vice versa). It could mean getting rid of little-used forums, or making a course simpler for members to engage with.

Don't be afraid to ask members what they want. Most will be constructive and supportive, and will have some great insights for you. You might want to run a regular members' survey, or simply use your forums / Facebook group / etc to ask for opinions.

Plan to review what's working and what isn't on a regular basis — maybe with a survey every six months.

Be careful not to overwhelm members with several different new initiatives at once. Try to introduce one thing at a time.

5 Myths about Membership Websites

There are some myths about membership web sites that just don't seem to go away.

Most of these myths serve as an excuse to laziness but there are also a lot of people that truly believe in them and view them as real obstacles.

Myth #1 – I Have To Be An Expert In What I Sell

This is one of the most common myths. People think that they won't sell anything because they are not experts on what they sell and they think that nobody will care about what they say.

The above is simple not true and it's very simple to find out the reason why.

Think about books, DVDs or other information products you've bought before, did you ever stop to think if they were the work of an expert? Did you care at all? Of course you didn't. The thing is, most people just care about if they will benefit from what they're buying, and they just care about if it'll improve their life in some way or not.

You can even create a membership web site about a topic you don't anything about. You can learn about it, simplify it and then teach it to people in your own unique way.

Myth #2 – I Have To Create Too Much Content

This is one is shared by two main groups of people, the extremely lazy and the ones that want to have everything. There's no solution for the first group but for the second group the solution is very simple. It is to always keep in mind that you create as much content as you purpose your product to have and that your product's quality doesn't depend on your content's quantity.

If you don't want to create a lot of content, don't try to offer everything and then some more on your membership web site.

Focus on one small aspect of your topic or niche, such as a beginner's perspective. Create just enough content for those but make sure it's really useful because that's what's really important.

Myth #3 – I Need To Create Content Forever

There are two main models of membership web sites, the fixed-term ones and unlimited content ones. The fixed-term type is where you have a limited amount of content, such as in a course or a training program that has a start date and an end date. This means that you can create all the content once and then re-use it again and again, revamping only the front-end as necessary.

These web sites are actually the most popular type of membership web site nowadays. They close their membership doors most part of the year and then use marketing techniques to get interested prospects on their lists and build their brand so that when they open the membership they already have members.

The unlimited content model is best used when there's an infinite need for content about a topic. In these cases, you really have to keep providing content on a regular basis but still you can even automate this. For example, you can spend one month creating content and then have it automatically delivered to your members for the next 6 months.

Myth #4 – The Technology Is Complicated

This used to be the case a few years ago but it is not true, anymore. Nowadays, it is as hard to create a regular web site as it is to create a membership web site. There are plenty of easy to use hosted solutions for non-techie people built especially with ease of use in sight.

Also, it's very cheap to start a membership web site because it doesn't require any big investments, just time and creativity.

Everybody can start a membership web site with extremely low overhead costs. Actually, selling information is one of the businesses with the lowest overhead.

Myth #5 – There Is Too Much Competition Already

This is another mind numbing myth that has the power to freeze anyone. The truth is, there will always be competition in every worthwhile niche.

That's completely normal and expectable because if there isn't any competition on a given niche it most likely means that there isn't any money to be made there.

You don't have to keep away from a niche you're passionate about just because it has some competition. The best strategy is to position yourself inside that niche and find your unique perspective, your unique way to deliver your content.

There is one exception to the rule though, a niche that you really should stay away from, especially if it's not your passion. It's the "how to make money online" or "internet marketing" niche. The problem with this niche is not even the super high competition; it's that people have lost their confidence in its products due to scams.

How To Create A Free E-Commerce Web Site

To engage in e-commerce, you MUST have a Web site as a place to promote products, like a book and, if you're serious, to sell both the printed book and a downloadable e-book!

Most small organizations and businesses do not need a super exotic site that costs a lot of money to create and maintain.

Neither should it beyond the capabilities of the individual to at least maintain the site with updates, calendar changes, newsletters, and the like without resorting to outside help.

From a practical standpoint, a Web site has to be capable of supplying you with the ability to create a custom look, and allow you to put in enough text, graphics, and linking to make it worthwhile.

What's more, it shouldn't be so complicated that you have to take a course in HTML programming in order to use it which, incidentally, is what many of the *free* offers require.

Of course, if the Web site doesn't do what you need it to do; it's not worth anything either so we set out with the following basic criteria understanding that the more exotic features could be added for a price, so based on our research, we recommend www.weebly.com.

At first glance, the Weebly Web site seems nothing special. But take a closer look and you'll discover an outstanding tool. It's simple, uncluttered and easy to use, and that's exactly what people with limited technical skills need it comes to creating your own Internet presence.

Added to this, Weebly's price/performance ratio is one of the best on the market: you can build up to 10 completely separate Web sites on the Pro plan.

Weebly.com is a Web site where anyone with basic word processing skills can create a Web site at no cost.

No special software is required, there are no hosting fees for the basic site and it only costs about $8 bucks a month to upgrade to the professional version which includes your own domain name and all of the professional features.

You can get a free video course on how to use Weebly for E-commerce at http://tinyurl.com/nkfaync.

The things you'll need on your Web site

An e-commerce site is NOT a 500 page brochure. It's basically the same information that we've traditionally put into an advertising sheet and order form.

The difference is that now it's electronic and easy to get to and use.

The basic elements include a page or two each with the following topics:

- About the business
- About the products and/or services
- How to order the products and/or services
- How to contact you
- Feedback form or BLOG

The shopping cart

If you're more interested in making money than tinkering with technology, you'll be happy to know that everything has been done for you so all you have to do is follow the directions to be successful.

Services like PayPal (www.paypal.com) provide everything you'll need to install a comprehensive shopping cart on your Web site including the ability to process the client's credit card order complete with tax, shipping, and a variety of other calculations if needed.

The big advantage of PayPal is that you're simply *brokering* the business and they actually handle the transaction for you.

This means you don't have to undergo financial vetting and since it's technically their processing efforts, it's free and they don't charge any fees or percentages except when a transaction is actually made.

At this point, you can plan on them keeping about three percent of the total transaction for their services.

Pay-Per-Download Service

There is a process called pay-per-download that allows the visitor to enter their credit card and download software, audio, video, and any form of electronically deliverable material

Recently a new service has been integrated into PayPal that provides this once very expensive service to virtually anybody who wants to use it. It's called E-Junkie and it's available from www.E-Junkie.com.

The philosophy is quite simple: *(Note: You'll still need your PayPal account to handle the money☺)*

- You register with E-Junkie
- You fill out their electronic shopping cart
- You upload the material to be sold via download

E-Junkie provides a link to the pay-per-download site so that you can put it on your Web page. When the visitor wants to buy a downloadable item, such as an e-book, they simply click on the button and they will be linked to the E-Junkie site.

When a purchase is made, PayPal charges the purchaser and subtracts a percentage of the purchase price as a handling fee.

They then direct the purchaser to a coded Web site address to download your e-book to their computer so that they can read it or print it at their discretion.

PayPal notifies you via e-mail that a transaction has occurred and the funds are available for you to transfer to your bank account.

This is the same system that iTunes and other related MP3 music systems and Kindle and other e-book distributors have capitalized on so extensively in the last few years.

The system has several different plans based solely on the amount of storage space you're going to use or the number of products you're going to offer, start at $5.00 per month and ramp up to $300 per month depending on the size or quantity.

The best part is that it's a fixed price whether you sell one or a million downloads each month so starting out with a free PayPal account and a $5.00 per month E-Junkie account will put you in the pay-per-download business for very little money Web site.

Once you've done, you'll have e-Published your e-book and made it available for sale.

The truly great part about this process is that once you've done the original work, you can keep selling the electronic files over and over again with no production, inventory, or shipping costs!

Here's a special note – If you're going to get into selling a lot of different physical goods and downloadable e-products, you'll want to check out the new e-commerce system from Weebly.

Weebly now offers a full e-commerce system for a total of $29 bucks per month and includes an unlimited pay-per-download feature plus a whole boatload of other features that you'd pay a lot more if you purchased tem separately.

QR Codes - The Easiest Way To Link People To Your Web site!

According to the 2014 statistics, over 68 percent of Americans own a smart phone or a tablet computer!

STOP the Presses!!! Before you print cards, ads, or any new promotional material, you MUST look into putting QR codes on them.

These are the little checkerboard squares that are popping up on everything from postcards to magazine ads to business cards to posters.

They are coded checkerboard codes that can be read by a smart phone or a tablet computer using a free app. Once scanned, the smart phone or tablet will automatically do what has been programmed into them, like instantly jump to your site.

The info about what they are is at http://tinyurl.com/3nbbylc

To create your own for FREE, go to www.QRStuff.com and use their free online code generator.

It's a JPEG graphic so all you have to do is copy and paste them onto anything and everything.

QR Code Readers To find a FREE QR Code Readers App for your Smart phone or tablet, go to your device's browser and type in: *FREE QR Reader app for XXX* where XXX is the name of your device.

You'll find a number of them so pick the one that seems to work best for you.

Here are two examples of QR codes for our materials. The first one is for our corporate Web site and the second one is for one of the author's YouTube demo videos.

How to Create a Membership Site with Weebly

Since we recommend, endorse (and use) the Weebly web site system, we recommend that you use their membership site add-one to make your life simple.

Sentry Login can convert your Weebly web site into a password protected site, and only members with appropriate passwords can access the member's only area.

It supports both paying and free memberships and setting this up is as simple as copy & paste!

Here are just some of Sentry Login's management features:

- Membership management system provides quick, easy web-based management of members who will log into your site using passwords
- Protects your web pages you want password protected from non-member access
- Member access fully automated by PayPal Subscriptions Instant Payment Notification (IPN)
- Sentry works with PayPal Subscriptions or any other processor (or none)
- Supports pay and free membership structures
- Unlimited number of members
- The cost of converting your Weebly site into a Members Only Site will cost you just $4.95 per month, and Sentry Login offers you a risk free trial for the first 7 days! This removes any financial risks from you so you can test drive their system.

Like Weebly, you can try Sentry with your web site today for free for 7 full days.

If you're not completely satisfied with the performance, seamlessness, and level of control it offers, cancel within that time and you won't be charged the monthly fee.

Click here to learn more about Sentry Login:
www.sentrylogin.com/sentry/index.asp

Drip Marketing

Drip marketing is a communication strategy that sends, or "drips," a pre-written set of messages to customers or prospects over time.

These messages often take the form of email marketing, although other media can also be used.

Drip marketing is distinct from other database marketing in two ways:

1. The timing of the messages follow a pre-determined course;
2.
3. The messages are dripped in a series applicable to a specific behavior or status of the recipient. it is also typically automated.

The most commonly used forms of drip marketing are:

1. E-mail marketing, due to the low cost associated with sending multiple messages over time. Email drip marketing is often used in conjunction with a Form (web) in a method called an auto responder.

2. Although more costly, direct mail software has been developed that enables drip marketing techniques using standard postal mail. This technology relies on digital printing, where low-volume print runs are cost justifiable, and the variable data can be merged to personalize each drip message.

3. The principles of drip marketing have been applied in many social media marketing tools to schedule a series of updates.

Why does drip marketing work so well?

Drip marketing utilizes and capitalizes on the famous Marketing Rule of 7. Never heard of it? Read on!

The Marketing Rule of Seven

It's an old concept, probably originating during the great depression.

Simply stated, The Marketing Rule of Seven is a reminder that your prospective buyer needs to hear or see your marketing message at least seven times before they buy from you.

Since the rule was written years ago, today that number is more likely to hover around 7.

The important thing in the Rule of Seven is not the number, but its meaning. Your prospect will need to hear and see your marketing message many MANY times before they decide to buy from you.

Here are the seven hurdles to your marketing that the drip addresses.

#1–Awareness: Your prospects need to first know you exist. And just putting your brand message out there once, isn't enough to break through their subconscious.

#2 - Need: Your prospect may not actually need what you're offering right now. That's okay. Until then, you'll be working on jumping the Awareness hurdle.

#3 – Like/Trust: Okay, your prospect now knows you exist and that you might have something that fixes their big problem. But they still aren't sure if they can actually trust you. That's because there are so many marketing messages out there that simply aren't true. You'll need to prove you're trustworthy, first. This is where all of your efforts to build a solid relationship kick in. Once you earn their trust, your prospect can move onto the next stage.

#4 – Price: Your prospect may be a little worried about the price. That's okay. When you show how much value you offer, this hurdle will fall away.

#5 – Time: Now that your prospect knows, likes and trusts you, and they know what you offer is a great value, they may need to do a little planning to work your fee into their budget. The higher your price, the longer this will take. For most people, if what you're selling is more than $50, it's not considered an impulse buy. Be prepared to wait a bit, but keep nurturing that relationship.

#6 – Choices: Depending on how much competition you've got, or even how many different options you're offering (yes, you can compete with yourself!), your prospect might be having a hard time choosing the perfect vendor.

#7 - Memory: Your prospect (like you) is a very busy person. Their To Do list is a mile long. So while they might have every intention of buying your thing, they might actually...um, forget.

When you look at this list, it's amazing that commerce even happens at all.

The point here is not to be disheartened, but to be enlightened.

If you know that decent response levels to any sort of marketing hover around 1 to 2%; AND you understand all of these hurdles to purchasing, you'll be better equipped to develop a marketing strategy that can go the distance.

Your branding and marketing efforts need to be repetitive and consistent. You cannot just run an ad one time and expect anyone to buy from you.

You've got to put together an integrated approach (e.g. use multiple methods that work together) so that your prospect hears and sees your brand and message many times.

Lead generation

Drip marketing can be used as a function of the lead generation and qualification process.

Specifically, drip marketing constitutes an automated follow-up method that can augment or replace personal lead follow-up.

Often called Auto responders, new leads are automatically enrolled into a drip marketing campaign with messaging relevant to the call-to-action from which the lead came. This is also known as lead nurturing.

Advantages include the automation and efficiency, as well as the continued ability for direct response.

Intelligent e-commerce sites, such as Dell, have integrated this form of drip campaign with add-on accessories and options.

The continued messaging is relevant to the contents that the shopper stopped short of purchasing, and continues to include direct response actions *(i.e. buy now).*

Disadvantages include the impersonal manner of follow-up. If not augmented with a traditional and personal follow-up method, this automated follow-up has a lower response rate than does personal sales.

The lowered response rate is often justified by the volume and efficiency with which leads can be generated and converted.

The sales process

Drip marketing is popularly applied as a sales tool, particularly in long sales-cycles (large ticket items or enterprise-level sales).

Whereas persistent follow-up can become a deterrent to closing the sale,

Drip Marketing methods offer the ability to remain top-of-mind, and even prompt action, without jeopardizing the relationship.

Selling Digital Goods Online (Pay-Per-Download)

One of the chief attractions of e-commerce is earning passive income — i.e. selling products or services instead of selling your own time.

A common way to do this is to sell digital goods such as eBooks, graphics, software, or anything that can be converted to digital format.

This is where digital goods services come in.

These services only take care of the payment, file storage, and download, and let you do the rest.

This means you can easily sell your products from your own web site, or through social networks.

First of all, let's see how those systems actually work.

Simply said, all these services let you upload some files, provide you with a link that you put on your site, and take care of the rest.

The customer flow usually looks something like this:

1. The client clicks the "Buy" button on your web site

2. The client briefly goes through the digital goods web site, and is automatically redirected to the payment processor

3. The client pays for your product with PayPal, Google Checkout, etc.

4. The client is then redirected to the digital goods service, where they can download the product

Payment Processors

Let's take a moment to look at that second step. Most digital goods services do not deal with the big credit card companies directly, but instead go through payment processors such as Paypal or Google Checkout.

This means that you need to take into account the additional fees charged by these companies (the standard fee for both service is a 2.9% charge plus a $0.30 fixed fee per transaction).

Instructions

Select a program to add the pay-per-download capability to your web site. There are several programs available that make it simple to set up a pay-per-download service for your customers.

Most of these programs are run through PayPal, but you can choose your payment preferences to also include credit cards.

One of the most commonly used download program is E-Junkie (www.ejunkie.com).

This service costs you $5 a month. They make it easy to use by coordinating your PayPal information for incoming payments, as well as providing links to add "Shopping Cart" buttons to your web site.

There are also no fees for how many purchases are made through your web site. This allows you to pay only the monthly fee.

Note: If you are using the Weebly web site system, they now have their own e-commerce store that you can add to your site that includes the pay-per-download feature thereby allowing you to sell digital goods.

You simply upload a picture, add a title for the product, enter a description and enter a price.

The system is linked to your payment processor, like PayPal, and the site allows you to upload and offer files up to 3 Giga Bytes in size.

Set up your downloads

Start by going through the sign-up process for the program you have chosen. Going through the program's setup process should be very easy.

Once you have set up payment through the web site, you can start adding your files to your site

This makes a file available for download to any customer who clicks on a link on your web site and automatically links to the specific file.

Each file you add to your web site will provide you with two links.

One link gives the option to add the file to the customer's shopping cart, while the other link shows "Buy Now."

When you post these links on your web site, they are shown as buttons to your customers.

Collect your payment.

When a customer clicks on the "Buy Now" button or makes a purchase from their shopping cart, they will enter their payment information based on the payment methods you have chosen to accept.

The payment processor through the server's web site will then verify that the payment information is valid and the money goes directly into your chosen account.

The customer is then given the chance to complete their purchased download.

Summary- The advantages of E-Commerce

1. Overcome Geographical Limitations

If you have a physical store, you are limited by the geographical area that you can service.

With an e-commerce web site, the whole world is your playground. Additionally, the advent of m-commerce, i.e., e-commerce on mobile devices, has dissolved every remaining limitation of geography.

2. Gain New Customers with Search Engine Visibility

Physical retail is driven by branding and relationships. In addition to these two drivers, online retail is also driven by traffic from search engines.

It is not unusual for customers to follow a link in search engine results, and land up on an e-commerce web site that they have never heard of. This additional source of traffic can be the tipping point for some e-commerce businesses.

a. Lower Costs

One of the most tangible positives of e-commerce is the lowered cost.

A part of these lowered costs could be passed on to customers in the form of discounted prices. Here are some of the ways that costs can be reduced using e-commerce:

b. Advertising and Marketing

Organic search engine traffic, pay-per-click, and social media traffic are some of the advertising channels that can be cost-effective.

c. Personnel

The automation of checkout, billing, payments, inventory management, and other operational processes, lowers the number of employees required to run an e-commerce setup.

d. Real Estate

This one is a no-brainer. An e-commerce merchant does not need a costly location.

e. Locate the Product Quickly

It is no longer about pushing a shopping cart to the correct aisle, or scouting for the desired product. On an e-commerce web site, customers can click through intuitive navigation or use a search box to immediately narrow down their product search. Some web sites remember customer preferences and shopping lists to facilitate repeat purchase.

f. Eliminate Travel Time and Cost

It is not unusual for customers to travel long distances to reach their preferred physical store.

Ecommerce allows them to visit the same store virtually, with a few mouse clicks.

3. Provide Comparison Shopping

E-commerce facilitates comparison shopping. There are several online services like www.shopathome.com, http://slickdeals.net, and www.bizrate.com that allow customers to browse multiple e-commerce merchants and find the best prices.

4. Enable Deals, Bargains, Coupons, and Group Buying

Though there are physical equivalents to deals, bargains, coupons, and group buying, online shopping makes it much more convenient.

For instance if a customer has a deep discount coupon for turkey at one physical store and toilet paper at another, she may find it infeasible to avail of both discounts. But the customer could do that online with a few mouse-clicks.

5. Provide Abundant Information

There are limitations to the amount of information that can be displayed in a physical store. It is difficult to equip employees to respond to customers who require information across product lines.

Ecommerce web sites can make additional information easily available to customers. Most of this information is provided by vendors, and does not cost anything to create or maintain.

6. Create Targeted Communication

Using the information that a customer provides in the registration form, and by placing cookies on the customer's computer, an e-commerce merchant can access a lot of information about its customers.

This, in turn, can be used to communicate relevant messages.

An example: If you are searching for a certain product on Amazon.com, you will automatically be shown listings of other similar products. In addition, Amazon.com may also email you about related products.

7. Remain Open All the Time

A physical store usually has hours and days when they are open. E-commerce stores are available to do business 24/7/365. From the merchant's point of view, this increases the number of orders they receive. From the customer's point of view, an *always open* store is more convenient.

8. Create Markets for Niche Products

Buyers and sellers of niche products can find it difficult to locate each other in the physical world. Online, it is only a matter of the customer searching for the product in a search engine.

One example could be purchase of obsolete parts. Instead of trashing older equipment for lack of spares, today we can locate parts online with great ease.

Promotion techniques for your program

Obviously, you have to have traffic to your e-commerce site so here are some of the best ways currently in use for driving that traffic to you.

Solo Ads and Ad Swaps

In super basic terms, a "***Solo Ad***" is when you (generally) pay someone to mail THEIR email list, on your behalf, with a recommendation and link to your free opt-in offer squeeze page.

An "***Ad Swap***" is the same idea only two people do it in exchange with each other to help each other out. (If one has a much larger list than the other, the one with the smaller list may need to mail twice, to send a fair amount of traffic.)

These two are basically the same, except that one is paying with an exchange and the other is paying with cash.

This type of advertising takes advantage of the relationship a marketer has with their list... that their list KLT's (knows, likes and trusts) them... to get some opt-ins for the other person.

This can be an incredibly powerful form of list building although there are a lot of variables that go into how good the results will be.

What Is Needed To Participate In Ad Swaps?

To start with, before you can do ANYTHING you have to have a few things in place....

Hosting – your squeeze/opt-in page has to be hosted somewhere on the internet

Auto-responder – this service allows you to capture a list and get good deliverability when you later send emails to them

An *"Ethical Bribe"* – this is the freebie you are exchanging with the visitor for their name and email address. This can be your own product/e-book or some kind of report or tips that you have the giveaway rights too.

A landing page (aka squeeze) for the other person to send traffic to for you.

And... either

1. Money to pay for a Solo Ad.

or

2. An existing double opt-in list you have a good relationship with to be able to mail an ad for the other person. (If the other person has a larger list than you do, you may also need to leverage your ability to promote to your twitter followers/etc. although these are technically not a list.)

Where to Find Ad Swaps and Solo Ads?

There are a number of places in the internet marketing world online that one can find potential people to do business with.

The Warrior Forum often has lots of people looking for/offering ad swaps, or selling Solo Ads.

Definitely be careful in there as you MUST find someone that has a good reputation or you could end up out some money.

One of the best ways however is within your own preexisting communities.

For example many of the tribe syndication communities are currently attempting to facilitate ad swaps among their members.

Often within your own niche and own private communities you can find groups offering ad swaps.
It is ALWAYS best to start these swaps in your existing communities (or communities you trust) so that the trust level is high and you feel comfortable promoting the other person.

Here are some great places to start looking at Solo ad promotions:

www.10dollarsoloads.com/
solo-ads.com/ultimate-advertising-package.html
Fiverr - www.fiverr.com
Freelancer http://www.freelancer.com/
PeoplePerHour http://www.peopleperhour.com/

Summary

Have your squeeze page together and need help finding an ad swap partner?

Feel free to talk to other people that reply to this thread and see if they wouldn't make good partners!

Want to learn more about Solo Ads? Pick up a copy of Solo Ad Revolution which I found really helpful at www.soloadrevolution.com/jv/.

Reseller Rights for E-Books

One of the most lucrative ways to generate revenues using e-commerce is to sell something that doesn't cost you anything, and there are a lot of e-books that you can obtain the resale rights to for free or a very low fee.

When you are given, or if you specifically purchase, resale rights for an e-Book, the original writer or creator of that publication has granted you limited permission to resell his e-Books to other people.

Several types of resale rights exist, each with varying degrees of flexibility regarding how you may resell the e-Books and what modifications, if any, you may make.

Ordinary Resale Rights (This is for everyday use)

Ordinary resale rights are the most common, most restrictive and least expensive. With ordinary eBooks resale rights, you will be granted the original author's permission to solicit and sell his work to other consumers but not to alter or manipulate the e-Books file or its contents in any way.

As the reseller, you will retain 100 percent of the profits from the sale of the e-Books. However, our resale rights only permit us to sell the e-Books to an end consumer and you cannot grant anyone else the right to sell the product.

- Master Resale Rights (This is what you want if you're offering a business opportunity as well as education and advice)

- Master resale rights are common and equally restrictive but typically are more expensive than ordinary resale rights. The same limitations exist regarding alterations and manipulation of the e-Books, as well as the ability to market and sell the publication.

- Master resale rights, however, also give you the ability to authorize additional resale rights licenses for that particular e-Book. You could grant permission for others to simply resell the e-Books with an ordinary resale license, or our specific master license might authorize us to transfer master resale rights.

- Private Label Rights (This is what you want if you're going to set up a fully branded series from your organization)

- Private label rights are less common than other types of reseller rights for e-Books, and such licenses usually cost the most. Few, if any, limitations exist on what you may do with the e-Books once these rights are granted.

Under a private label resell agreement, the content of the e-Books can be altered in any way, including removal of the original author's name. You could essentially pass off an e-Book as our own work and edit the piece to suit our needs or goals.

Rebranding Rights

Rebranding rights are common, and the cost is typically higher than other reseller licenses but less than private label rights. Unlike ordinary and master reseller rights, rebranding agreements usually allow the license holder to edit only certain chapters, sections or other aspects of an e-Book.

For example, the original author's name can be replaced, the e-Books title can be changed and affiliate links within the book can be substituted with those belonging to the licensee. However, the bulk of the actual content of the work must remain complete and intact.

Sites with e-Books to consider:

- www.bookswealth.com/
- www.seymourproducts.com/
- www.sandfinder.net/
- www.internetmarketingzoom.com/
- www.ossface.co/
- www.plrebookfoundry.com/
- www.masterresalerightsebooks.com/offline-business-ebooks.html
- www.idplr.com/
- www.resaleproducts.net/catalog/Business-158-1.html
- http://e-library.net/
- http://craftkeys.com/online/online-business-ebook/
- www.gutenberg.org

For example, here's a really great 1883 book about printing, paper, ink, and creating recipes that's free to download:

www.gutenberg.org/files/32400/32400-h/32400-h.htm

Next, we have included a FREE downloadable e-book written by the famous P.T. Barnum that we cleaned up and reformatted as an example of what you can acquire and sell without incurring a lot of expense for the products.

Barnum was, arguably, one of the greatest promoters the world has ever seen and his real world philosophies and advice are still as valuable today as they were when he wrote them down over 100 years ago.

This came from the Gutenberg project and the disclaimer at the end of the book is what allows you to actually sell the e-book even though it was originally offered for free.

Web Site URL: http://tinyurl.com/k8ab87a
Password: CPM7MFR

Disclaimer

This eBook is for the use of anyone anywhere at no cost and with almost no restrictions whatsoever.

Anything you have paid for it is strictly for the efforts involved in making it available to you in its current format and not for the content itself.

You may copy it, give it away or re-use it under the terms of the Project Gutenberg License included with this eBook or online at www.gutenberg.org.

How to create an e-mail marketing plan

Reproduced by permission from Mailchimp
http://static.mailchimp.com/web/guides/how-to-create-an-email-marketing-plan/package/how-to-create-an-email-marketing-plan.pdf

You know you want to do some email marketing. Or, perhaps more accurately, you feel like you're supposed to do some email marketing. Where to start? An "email marketing plan" sounds complicated, intimidating, and time-consuming.

Besides, you're too busy running your business to deal with such a thing, right? This guide's for you.

You're smart to explore email marketing for your business. For some perspective, email marketing has three times as many user accounts as Twitter and Facebook combined. Combined with social media, that impact is even greater. Done smartly, email marketing drives conversions, increases ROI, and gives you a way to speak to your customers interests specifically.

An email-marketing plan isn't as hard to put together as you might think. In this guide, we'll walk you through the most important steps, highlight real-life case studies along the way, and give you everything you need to know to get started.

Step One: Define Your Readers

Before you start designing, writing, and sending campaigns, you should define your audience. Once you get a grasp on the people reading your emails, it'll be much easier to decide what to say to them.

If you have subscribers on your list already, who are they? One way to determine this is how they signed up. If they subscribed during checkout, they're customers. But if they found you through your web site or in public (fairs, trade shows, etc.), they're more of a general audience.

If you don't have subscribers yet, who is your target audience? How will you find these people, and what do you envision they'll want to read in your emails?

Perhaps you're a publisher or blogger. In that case, your subscribers are going to be interested in your written content. If you're a retailer, subscribers will want to know about your new products or how they can better use products they've already purchase from you. If you're somewhere in between, your audience is likely made up of enthusiasts of your brand.

Rooftop Comedy lands somewhere in that third category. The San Francisco-based company sells comedy albums, produces festivals, and record stand up all over the United States.

With their "Clip of the Week" emails, Rooftop has found an entertaining, kind-of-sneaky way to delight their customers with the humorous brand they've come to know and love while also reminding them that they've got things for sale.

Step Two: Determine Your Content

Now that you know who you're talking to, it's time to think about what you're going to say to them. This is your content. Think about why this audience signed up, then focus on delivering that to them.

It can be helpful to outline general content types that you might include in each email campaign. Later, as you're putting together your newsletter, this outline will be a handy reference to make sure you're staying on track.

The Atlanta Rollergirls keep a content list:

- Upcoming events
- Recaps/photos from past events

Popular posts on Facebook, Twitter, blog News coverage Derby 101 (an in-depth look at rules/strategy) Player profiles

Each month, they choose 1-4 pieces of content from the list to create a campaign.

Think about what content you're already creating that you might want to share to make sure your subscribers don't miss it. A popular tweet, a Facebook post, an article about your company—these are things your readers will likely find interesting. Think also about what content you'd like to create exclusively for this audience. Reward them for caring about what you do.

MonkeyWrench is MailChimp's quarterly newsletter that showcases app updates, user case studies, and relevant email-marketing news. We also include funny links, videos we've made about our customers, and more.

Tips for creating and gathering content

Your content is the most important part of your newsletters. Here are some tips for making and gathering compelling content that will speak to your readers:

1. Treat your readers like VIPs.

People who subscribe to your email list are so into you that they've given you permission to their inboxes. Honor this permission and dedicated fandom by letting them be the first to know about new products or sales. Give them access to special benefits as subscribers.

Clothing retailer Billy Reid goes one step further, sending exclusive sales to its readers with the highest member-activity ratings.

2. Keep it useful.

Think about which emails you open and which you delete right away. You don't open an email that doesn't benefit you in some way. Make sure the content of your newsletters are giving your subscribers something they didn't have before.

"The reader comes first," Peter Cooper told MailChimp. "Without happy and loyal readers, you have a weak publication, whether it's a magazine, newspaper, or an email list. The majority of email newsletters are all about linking to a company's own projects, products and news. I think it's pretty rare that they delight their readers."

3. Show some personality.

No one wants to read a dry, boring newsletter that drones on and on and doesn't even say anything about zzzzzzzzzz.. Inject some personality. Chances are, your voice, tone, and sense of humor are all important reasons why your customers signed up in the first place.

Try to write the same way you'd speak to one of these customers. And who knows? Maybe your lighthearted, humorous emails will help you raise a whole bunch of money.

4. Keep it short.

Most people are bombarded with emails every day. Keep your newsletters short, easy to digest, and to the point. If you'd like to include a longer piece, feature the first paragraph or so and link away to the rest. Allow your readers the opportunity to scan quickly, if necessary.

5. Get inspired.

Apps like Pocket, Evernote, and Pinterest are great for saving, organizing, and accessing content to use in your campaigns later.

Additionally, our inspiration board features hundreds of elegant, thoughtful email examples from MailChimp customers who are great at email marketing.

Step Three: Determine Your Sending Frequency and Goals

Not all sending frequencies are created equal. Some users, like Dave Pell or Quartz, send on a daily basis because that's the point of their content. Others, like Longreads or Rooftop, send on Fridays, like a little e-gift for the weekend.

Ultimately, you have to decide what works best for you and your customers.

We recommend you email at least monthly, but don't feel the need to commit to that immediately. Feel free to skip a month if you have anything truly useful to say. Remember, content first.

Be careful not to skip more than a couple months in a row, however, as some subscribers may forget they opted in and may report you for spam. Remember also to look ahead and plan accordingly for holidays, events, and the like.

From there, decide what you'd like to get out of your email marketing. Are you looking to send traffic to your web site? Help promote sales? Increase traffic at events? Set goals like these for your campaigns, then keep track of your progress over time.

Step Four: Make a Schedule

Not everyone is going to send on a regular schedule, but for a lot of senders, having a timeline is helpful, if only because it gives writers, designers, and managers a deadline to work toward.

If you have several people working on your team, consider MailChimp's Multi-User Accounts feature and other collaboration tools.

Your email-marketing schedule will vary, of course, depending on industry, type of content, sending frequency, and so on.

But here's an example of how you might plan out your campaigns:

Day 1: Jot down content topics, art ideas, basics for your upcoming newsletter.

Day 2: Write out what you'd like to say about each topic, pull photos or art into a folder.

Day 3: Log in to MailChimp and create your campaign. Proofread for errors and grammar. Send a test campaign to yourself and at least one co-worker.

Day 4: Send your campaign.

Resources

We hope this guide has helped you create a comprehensive email-marketing plan for your business.

If you have questions about our application, feel free to contact MailChimp's support team.

The Concept of Web Traffic!

The most common term used when speaking about any Internet marketing topic is *traffic* and basically it means the number of visitors that arrive at a particular site.

When a Web site says that it has traffic of a million per month, it means that a million people visit that particular site each month.

Things you should understand as an Internet marketer:

Traffic or hits, per se, is not useful to the Internet marketer. It is the unique traffic that counts.

The people that click on your Web site link are hardly of any use to you. To make your business a success, you need these people to take some specific action.

You need them to download an e-book, subscribe on your Web site or pay and buy a product, etc.

Getting and Doing

In the world of practical and successful business, you will encounter two primary components:

- Getting the business and

- Doing the business.

The truth is that although many people are very good at doing something, like writing for example, they are not good at getting the business, which is selling their books.

The success in e-commerce comes primarily from getting the business or the marketing efforts and that's what the hot traffic is all about – getting the business.

Hot and Cold Traffic

The concept of hot and cold traffic will soon become very important to you.

Simply put, people who just arrive on your Web site and go away doing nothing are known as HITS, considered cold traffic, and are of no use to you.

Several years ago an advertising executive said that H.I.T.S. is an acronym that stands for ***how idiots track success***.

His logic was that knowing the number of hits or unspecified visitors you get on a Web site is basically irrelevant because you don't know anything about the visitors, what they were interested in, where they came from, or what they would like to do once they're on your Web site.

Cold traffic comes from simple untargeted methods such as Google searches. These people have probably got your Web site when they were looking for a particular keyword on Google.

They didn't not have any inclination to visit your Web site specifically; they just turned up, and visited your Web site without any expectation. The conversion rate of these people is very low.

Needless to say, it's hot traffic that you should be striving for, and hot traffic comes on your Web site through some targeted methods!

They might have arrived because of some of your efforts that are described below.

Naturally, these are the people who mean the most for you in terms of business prospects.

They come to your Web site with some expectation, so you can hope for some business from them too.

Monetizing The Traffic

Monetizing means converting your traffic into money. In Internet marketing, bringing in hot traffic to your Web site is the objective and the key to success is to monetize this traffic.

How to Increase Hot Traffic for Free

You can build your own hot traffic and visitors to your Web site without even spending a penny.

Optimize your Web site to be search-engine friendly. Submit it to various search engines and directories. In addition to major search engines such as Google, Yahoo, Ask, Bing and MSN, it's worth submitting to lesser known Web directories even though it's cold traffic.

Make sure your title, description head, and header html tags accurately convey the subject of your site; search engine algorithms use these as keywords to categorize your site and direct relevant traffic.

Spread the word about your site by submitting it to affiliate program directories and contacting the owners of related sites.

Create a links page that will contain the links to other non-competing Web sites in the same industry. Contact the owners of other Web sites with your proposal to exchange links.

Post in forums. Visit the online discussion forums where people in your target market like to gather. Post useful responses to people's questions, and include a link to your Web site at the end of your post next to your name.

Comment on blogs. Visit other people's blogs on the topic related to your Web site. Most blogs allow you to add comments about the issues being discussed. Add insightful comments about the blog topics, and leave your Web site link. Your comment and your link will permanently remain on the blog Web site.

Create an e-mail "signature" with your name, your Web site address and a short tag-line describing the main benefit of your site. Set your e-mail program to automatically add your signature to every e-mail that you send.

Look into traffic exchanges. There are many types of traffic exchanges but the idea is the same—you team up with other Web masters, and they send you traffic in exchange for you sending them traffic. Search the Web for *traffic exchange* to find those services.

Create something of value that people will pass around like a report with useful information that you allow people to give away. Of course, the pass-around item will include your advertisement and your link, spreading the word about your Web site. This is a *viral* strategy.

Write articles on the topic related to your Web site, and include a link to your site in your author bio. Submit your articles to article directories, and allow people to publish your article in their newsletters and Web sites. People will read them and visit your Web site. The best part is that people who read your articles will regard you as an expert, and they will be much more likely to buy from you when they go to your Web site.

Use accurate keywords for your content. The point of keywords is that they are the terms most people looking for your offerings by topic will search by. Check those with free Google terms and use the most popular relevant one in your title—a descriptive title to let them know right away what it is if it's a word with multiple meanings. Don't overdo it, or you look like you're trying to spam Google. Just use the keywords naturally when describing the topic.

Start an e-zine for your Web site. When people read each issue they'll be reminded to revisit your Web site. Submit it to all the free e-zine directories on the internet.

Start your own online discussion community. It could be an online message board, e-mail discussion list or chat room. When people get involved in your community, they will regularly return to communicate with others.

Advertise your site at free classified ad sites. There are many of these on the net. Some of the more popular ones are craigslist, inetgiant, freeadvertisingforum, and gumtree.

Join www.freesafelists.com. These are lists of subscribers who have opted-in to send and receive e-mails to each other. You can instantly reach thousands of people by sending out e-mails, and you don't have to worry about receiving spam complaints because everyone on the list has opted-in to receive e-mails.

Constantly update content on your Web page. Having a topic specific news section is a great deal for search engines especially.

Update your Facebook status to let your friends know every time you update your blog and create a Facebook fan page. Your friend's friends will see when they join the fan page or comment on your status.

Submit your Web site to top social bookmarking sites to create a link to your Web site.

Sign up to Yahoo answers and leave great helpful comments to questions people are asking for, leaving a link back to your site with more helpful tips on it.

Use word of mouth. Tell everyone you know about your Web site.

Promoting and Linking Your Site

Now that you've completed your Web site, you are part of the trillion page electronic library known as the World Wide Web and are now faced with the same problem as everybody else who has a Web site up and running: How are people going to find you?

For all the hype and rhetoric that has been put forth about being found by search engines, buying search words, and all the magic tricks for getting to the top of the search engines, the very best procedure for having your Web site found is to get maximum exposure for your site.

Simply stated this means that you are better off using conventional advertising that your clients or potential clients are currently experiencing and responding to for notifying them that you have a Web presence.

If you question the validity of this process think about every place where you see URLs listed. These include places like:

- The ends of television programs
- Announcements on radio
- Magazine advertisements
- Billboards
- Bus benches
- Buses
- And people's rear windows.

For as important as search engines are, the statistics tell us that most people have never been properly trained in the use of search engines. Consequently when they're looking for you, they're likely to find somebody else.

If that seems counterproductive to all the work that you've done, it probably is, so the answer to it is to make sure that your potential clients or visitors to your Web site type in your URL instead of looking through a for a generic list of responses from a search engine.

Once you have established your Web presence, make sure that every time you change your letterheads, business cards, or any other advertising material, that you include the Web address so the people will know exactly how to find your site.

This whole concept of initially promoting and driving people back to your Web site is part of a time honored and proven method of advertising and promotion called the two-step process.

The two-step process relies on small initial advertising to pique people's curiosity while simultaneously referring them to a method for obtaining additional information that will lead them to make the buying decision, whatever that turns out to be.

The example shown is from Popular Mechanics magazine, a 137-year-old publication. The ads are small space ads that appear in the back of the magazine and lack all of the power and glory necessary to get people to make a purchase.

They do however, contain enough information and graphics to get people's curiosity aroused enough to request additional information.

Traditionally an ad like the one on the left for micro wireless cameras would have referred people to a mailing address to request a paper catalog. Notice that neither the phone number nor the snail mail address appears but instead contains the URL which will allow people to instantly go to the camera's Web site and view the catalog with all of its details and pictures including the ability to make a purchase.

The Quickest and Easiest Way To Link People To Your Web Site!

According to the 2014 statistics, over 67 percent of Americans own a smart phone or a tablet computer!

OK—STOP the Presses!!! Before you print cards or any more promotional material, you MUST look into putting QR codes on them.

These are the little checkerboard squares that are popping up on everything from postcards to magazine ads to business cards to posters.

They are coded checkerboard codes that can be read by a smart phone or a tablet computer using a free app. Once scanned, the smart phone or tablet will automatically do what has been programmed into them.

Here's the overview about what they are and how they work.
http://tinyurl.com/3nbbylc

To create your own for FREE, go to www.QRStuff.com and use their free online code generator. It's a JPEG graphic so all you have to do is copy and paste them onto anything and everything.

QR Code Readers To find a FREE QR Code Readers App, go to your device's browser and type in: FREE QR Reader app for XXX where XXX is the name of your device. You'll find a number of them so pick the one that seems to work best for you.

Here are two examples of QR codes for our materials. The first one is for our corporate Web site and the second one is for one of my YouTube demo videos.

The operative statement here is: “new tools, old rules.”

The summation of this approach is simply stated by saying that we are better served advertising our Web sites in places where we are reasonably sure that our prospective clients are going to be able to see the advertisement and respond to it rather than dropping it into a massive bucket of millions of URLs and hoping that the prospective client fishes ours out.

Ask Jeeves Goes Bananas

Ask Jeeves usea a real bananna-gram to tell people where to go

Are dot-com ads taking over the world? Ask Jeeves.

The search engine recently upped the ad ante with stickers on 100 million bananas nationwide. Instead of peeling Chiquita or Dole labels off produce, consumers are confronted with Jeevsian consultations on a variety of *affaires bananes.*

“We wanted to place an ad where it's really relevant to people,” spokeswoman

out with mess
Christmas t
But eve
has his li
turned aw
national br
that wanted
on melons,” he
there was a condo
that wanted to advertise
We just didn't think it was appro

Ask Jeeves uses a real bananna-gram to tell people where to go

Probably one of the most extreme examples of this was being done by Ask Jeeves (now ASK.com), and Jell-O. Both of these organizations have made arrangements to put peel and stick labels on the sides of bananas thereby creating a banana-gram with an ad that notifies people that they are available on the Web.

For as ludicrous as this may appear, the process is actually quite effective. Another example that we have observed is e-diets.com utilizing the billboard space that’s built into supermarket shopping carts to advertise their weight control programs.

Online Directories

Another excellent and somewhat overlooked place to promote your Web site is in the online telephone directories.

There are a variety of them shown in the box on the right and you'll notice that these are the electronic equivalent of Yellow Pages

Online Directory Sites
www.bigfoot.com
www.infospace.com
www.switchboard.com
www.whowhere.com
www.bigbook.com

Most of them are free for users and are actually paid for by the advertisers who put billboards along the directory sites.

Unlike paper Yellow Pages, which cost hundreds perhaps even thousands of dollars to list in, these sites are free and offer you an additional opportunity to gain exposure.

The logic behind using these directories is that we are never sure where the potential visitor client is going to look for us in since these listings are free, why not take advantage of.

Why The Search Words Are Important

When the Web was originally being developed and implemented, one of the initial concerns was how users of the Web were going to be able to find the content that they wanted.

Since the Web is the electronic equivalent of a huge library, the original developers looked to the time-honored Dewey decimal system as a technique for indexing and finding content on the Web. Unfortunately, the Dewey decimal system doesn't work for the system that we know as the Web so the developers looked for alternative.

After considerable deliberation they concluded that there was no simple way to search the vast array of content although the titles of the Web sites could be done relatively easily using a process similar to the Dewey decimal system.

As a trade-off, the developers decided that the first thing that any search tool or search engine would look at would be a series of key words that the

Web site developers would apply to their site that would describe the overall purpose and content of the site.

These words are technically known as meta tags, although they are often referred to as keywords, index words, link words, and profile words.

Before we proceed further, it's important to note that although the search engines look at the meta tags first, each of the search engines has their own proprietary techniques, which are constantly being changed and updated, to search, link, list, and index every Web site on the Web.

If you are concerned about how the search engines actually go about the in-depth search process, check out www.searchenginewatch.com, the premier site on the Internet that explains how each engine is currently searching and indexing Web sites.

As you read this detailed report, you'll notice that it changes from month to month and each site has their own proprietary process for determining what they think is the most important content or listing element to get the searcher's information back in a hierarchical index.

There is a long and sordid history involved with the concept of changing your meta tags so that you get on top of the search engines.

When the dotcom bubble burst in Y2K, the search engine's had to reexamine and redefine how they were going to allow Web site developers to list and link with their sights.

Prior to the dotcom crash which redefined the economics of the Internet, you could purchase software that will allow you to change modify, alter, and resubmit your meta tags and descriptions as often as you wanted at no charge.

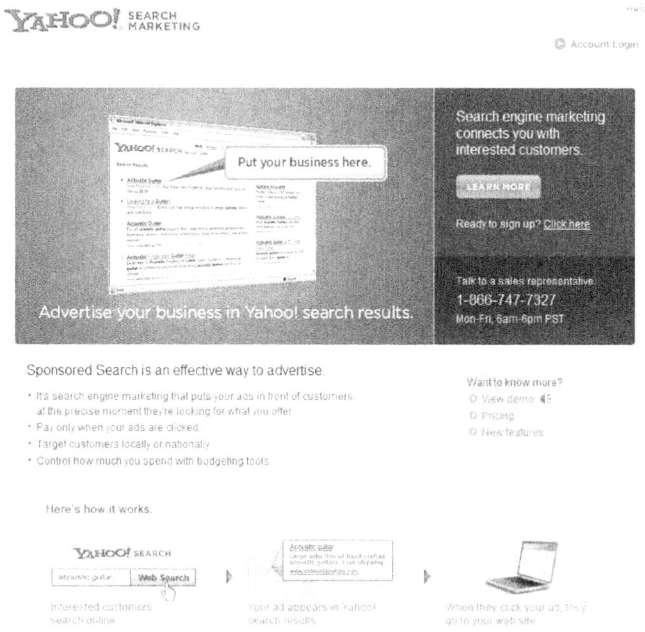

The logic behind these rapid changes were spurred on by the theory that if you selected meta tags, monitored your Web site, and discovered that you weren't getting the hits you wanted or weren't being listed high enough up on the search engine lists, that the fastest way to remedy this was to change the indexing words so that the next time somebody performs a search you would end up higher on the list.

The problem with this logic was, and is, that it requires an inordinate amount of time to analyze and make changes on the Web site. Couple this with the technical support that was constantly being requested and the complaints that were being received by the search engines by people who have decided that they should be listed higher than they actually were, the search engines decided to abandon the *no charge* process in favor of an optional free or fee system.

The basic system that most of the major search engines currently follow is that if you want to have control over how fast you are indexed by the engine and how you are actually listed; there is an associated fee for each time you make a change or a modification.

Most of the major search engines charge between $200 and $300 each time you make a change which means that if you are constantly monitoring and modifying your site, it could be a very expensive proposition.

Today most Web developers simply select and install meta tags on their Web sites, publish them, and let the search engines perform a process called auto spidering. This auto spidering or auto indexing by the search engines is a free service that puts your Web site and its meta tags into the search engine's database.

The down side to the free listing services is that indexing or reindexing of your site, along with the way that you are listed in the search engines database, is strictly a function of the search engine and you have no control over the process. The reality is that most people don't benefit from constantly reindexing their Web site so the bulk of all the Web sites available have probably been auto spidered.

Selecting Meta Tags

Remember that the first thing that we look at when we travel through the stacks on the library is the Dewey decimal system on the spine of a book. Search engines begin their search by looking at the meta tags that have been placed on the Web site. After that, depending on the algorithms and the process that the search engine has chosen to use, other elements of the Web site are considered and then placed on the retrieved list.

For purposes of example in selecting meta tags, let's assume that we own a company that is in the business of toilet repair.

Toilet

- **Synonyms** bath, bathroom, latrine, lavatory, rest room, washroom, water closet

Logic dictates that for our meta tags we should use the words toilet, repair, and the two words as a phrase toilet and repair to cover all the possible combinations.

This logic works until somebody decides to type in a word like plumbing or some word other than toilet to describe a toilet.

The inequity occurs when somebody types a word into the search engine that does not match the meta tags on our Web site at this point, our site does not match the search and we don't end up on the retrieval list.

One of the fastest and simplest ways to help ensure that your found in the meta tag search is to use Merriam-Webster's Web site at www.M-W.com and invoke the use of their free electronic thesaurus.

Simply type in the words you have selected and let that thesaurus pick all of the common synonyms that are in use today. Once you have the synonyms, simply cut and paste them into your meta tags string.

Meta Tag Selection Tips

Customer surveys are best. How we describe our Web site and the words that we'd use to find our site are not necessarily the same as the visitors. If you can ask friends, relations, and clients what words they would use, you'll have a much broader array than the ones you select

Include abbreviations and initials. There are a great many abbreviations and initials that we use on a daily basis instead of actually saying or writing the formal name of the organization. If there are initials or acronyms that are used to describe your organization or any of the products or services that you offer, be sure to include them in the meta tags

Firm name. Even though the name of your organization or firm will appear on the Web site itself, the first search conducted by the search engine is on the meta tags and having your organization's name listed there will help ensure that you end up on the retrieval list.

Foreign words. The Web is worldwide and is used by a variety of people who speak different languages. If you believe that your Web site, and the material contained in it, is of interest to others who speak a language other than English, it would probably be in your best interest if you were to provide the meta tags in their native language.

In order to do this all you have to do is go to www.translate.google.com and

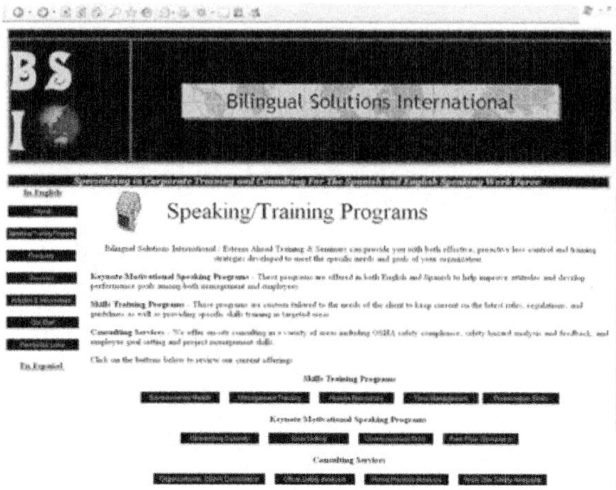

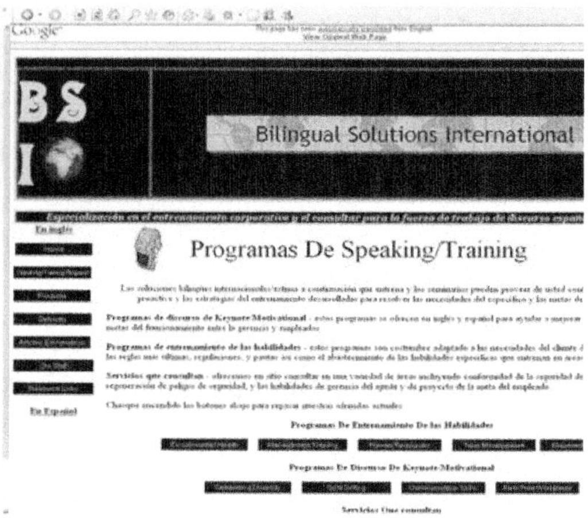

English | Spanish

click on their language tools.

Google offers a free service of translating words, phrases, and entire Web pages from your language to any other language covering a variety of possibilities that will help you to make sure that you get found by persons who are looking in another language.

We have included examples of a Web site that is primarily in English, **Bilingual Solutions International**, and another example of what it looks like after it has been translated into Spanish by **Google**.

Google also offers complete Web page translation so if the person searching for you find your content and does not speak English, they can simply type the URL into the Web page translation service of a good Web site and have it translated into whatever language they prefer. Conversely, if you during the course of your searching find a Web site that is not in English, you can have it converted to English.

It has been noted by several linguists that the translation service provided by Google is not grammatically perfect. However, the translation is rapid and 80 to 90 percent effective so that all that is required to make a grammatically correct its final editing.

We have also included an example of translating the author's site from English into Spanish for an immediate reference.

Common misspellings—one of the cleverest things that you can do is to take the most common meta tags used to describe your site and investigate the most common misspellings.

Once you have these common misspellings, add them to your meta tags so that visitors who misspell the meta tags still get a lock to your site

A More Sophisticated Approach to Creating Meta Tags

Most users of the Internet have received one or more outrageous offers to either buy a report or pay for services that guarantee to put their site on top of the search engines.

Although these reports are probably true and accurate, the advertising leaves out the amount of time and effort required on a weekly or daily basis needed to make sure that your listing efforts are keeping pace with the efforts of the search engines to stay ahead of the hackers and other miscreants who are trying to scam the system.

On the other hand, no matter what articles, hype, or marketing materials you're read about being found by the search engines, the one thing that **EVERYBODY** agrees on is that the first and most important thing you **MUST** do to your Web site is select and add the *meta tags* because this is the first place that the search engines look and list.

The basic concept says that if we type a word like my name, **"Mike Rounds"**, into the search box on Google or Yahoo, I'll appear somewhere on the list of site that Google finds that have the same words.

Right now, if you perform the search as listed on Google, there are two primary listings; the former Governor of South Dakota and me, and each of us have five of the top ten listings.

If you add the word *speaker* so that the search reads "Mike Rounds speaker", I have 10 of the top ten listing all by myself plus several pictures.

If you type in "Mike Rounds governor", he has 10 of the top ten listing all by himself.

Is that cool or what?

Are you beginning to get the idea that the meta tags are important to being found?

The key to success, an demonstrated in the example using my name, is to find and add as many possible combinations of words and phrases as possible to your meta tags so that when an unknown person types what they think they're looking for into a search box, that you've anticipated their words and have them on your site.

It's kind of like fishing with a net and obviously, the bigger the net, the more fish you'll catch.

Getting Found—Advanced Keyword Research

Potential viewers are most likely going to find your site by using the Google search tool so it makes logical sense, if we want to be found, to include the words and phrases that the viewer is most likely to type in to find related information about their topic of choice.

Whatever you're offering, it has a name or names that people would use to locate it. Unfortunately, not everyone calls the same thing by the same name or term so it's our job to come up with as many different terms as we can that the potential buyer might type into a search engine to find us.

The first step is to start with an electronic thesaurus and find all of the synonyms for whatever word we think is the most commonly used.

Another free site is www.synonyms-for.com and is a great place to start. For example, if you ask for a synonym for *wrench*, this is what you'll get:

- **Wrench**
- **Tool (part of speech: noun)** arc welder, auger, awl, axe, back saw, ball-peen hammer, band saw, bench drill, bow saw, buzz saw, calipers, chain saw, chisel, circular saw, claw hammer, cold chisel, coping saw, crosscut saw, crowbar, drill, drill press, edger, emery wheel, file, gouge, grapnel, grindstone, hacksaw, hammer, handsaw, hatchet, hedge trimmer, hoe, jackknife, jigsaw, jointer, keyhole saw, knife, lathe, level, lug wrench, machete, mallet, miter box, monkey wrench, pick,

Pretty cool, huh?

There's another great site at http://soovle.com/ that will show you a kind of "synonym search" based on the major search engines like Google, Bing, and Yahoo as well as YouTube.

Obviously, not all of these will apply to what you're doing but it's better to have more than you need than less.

After all, you don't know what kind of educational background or what's just been happening in the potential buyer's life that that might cause them to use one of these words to describe a tool that tightens and loosens bolts.

What you're doing here is creating a sales funnel with a **matrix of words** that you think (or hope) that the person searching Google will type in to find more information about a particular subject and the wider the mouth of the funnel, the more captures you'll make.

Using Google Tools

In addition to figuring out what people are calling something, it's in our best interest to see just how many people are actually searching for a particular term that relates to the topic.

The most comprehensive process is to use the **Google Keyword Tool** which instantly shows us demand for a specific word, phrase, or related (similar) word, keyword, or phrase along with both the global and local search for those words.

To use this tool, simply enter a word or phrase, and click on the search button. The Google Keyword Tool shows you the term you entered, along with several other related terms.

Google can effectively show you demand as they publish the Global Monthly searches for the respective term in the Google search engine. Here's the free lookup site:

http://tinyurl.com/2fu9n5o

Here are four ways to take advantage of the Google Keyword Tool:

Identify the words and phrases that potential clients use

This tool shows you what is on a potential customer's mind when they look for something on the Web.

This means you'll get a statically researched and reported set of words that people are using to find something related to what you're offering.

In addition to providing keywords for your sites, this can help when writing marketing copy or slogans as you can see the popular terms on someone's mind in regards to a given keyword.

If you use terms that have good results, but not the best, you'll see what users are thinking about when they are looking for a given product or service.

Compare the demand between two terms

You often may not know which of two terms will make more of an impact with users. When comparing the search volume for two keywords, you can instantly see which one has more popularity and demand on the Web.

Are people more interested in blue baseball caps or red baseball caps? Google can tell us in five seconds!

See related terms for any term

When you enter in "credit card", Google will show you tons of related terms.

You can see, for example, several other terms that users search for which include the keyword credit card.

This of course is valuable data as you can drill down deeper into a given term to learn more specific things users are looking for which include that given term.

Find new terms and ideas which have demand behind them

The Google Keyword Tool helps identify new terms, which you may not have previously realized, have demand behind them.

For example, you can type in a slew of keywords, and find related terms, and then quickly export the data to see a list of keywords and the demand behind them.

In doing this, you will probably notice new keywords and new areas of interest in your niche that you may not have known previously existed

There's a complete online FREE video course by Google on how to select keywords at: http://tinyurl.com/lj8eggz

If you expand the information available by clicking on the topic, you'll see a magnifying glass that will get you to the Google insights page which has a lot of unbelievable statistics about the searches for the terms you have requested.

If you click on the topic itself, you'll be directed to the entire list of pages that Google has found from the search.

Types of keywords:

Keywords related to your niche topic

- Use them in your titles and keywords
- Note: Keywords found in videos also appear in Google

Research current event keywords related to your niche topic

Research "upward trends" to see where your niche market is going.

Foreign words

As noted above, if you think that your goods and services might be of interest to people whose primary language in NOT English, it will be useful for you to also list your key words in another language as well.

Google has a FREE toolkit for accomplishing this function at www.translate.google.com.

This toolkit will allow you to enter the keywords in English and convert them to the languages shown above. Once they are converted, you can add them to your list of key words when you post your Web site.

Adding Meta Tags To Your Web Site

If you're using one of the major Web authoring software packages, Like Weebly, it will probably have a box for you to type the meta tags and it'll handle the HTML conversion and insertion for you.

If it doesn't or the instructions don't make sense to you, this may be the only time that you will ever have to get into the HTML code of your Web site because meta tags are written and added to the Web site in HTML code.

The fastest, easiest and cheapest way to convert the meta tags to an HTML string is to go to www.promotionworld.com/tools/meta.php. They have a free HTML meta tag string writer that allows you to put in your site description and the meta tags. By simply clicking on a tab, the software will write the HTML string for you.

When you publish your Web site to your server, the meta tags will have been inserted and published along with the content and the search engines will index the site as a part of their normal routine.

How to Create A Free E-Commerce Web Site

Although there have been ways to create a free Web site since the Web began, few of the methods were really free, easy, or comprehensive enough to do most people any good.

When someone says "it's free", there's some kind of a catch because somebody has to pay for it.

Fortunately with some of the newer renditions of free Web site systems, the *free* is simply being bombarded with a bunch of advertising for paid programs when you're downloading the application, advertising banners on the site, or the absence of more desirable features like audio, video, and embedded files that are only available as a premium upgrade.

That being said, there is still enough power and functionality in many of the free systems to make them well worth considering.

Web site builders can offer you an easy way to build, design and organize your Web site without having to use complicated computer code. Many hosting providers include free Web site builders in their hosting plan but some builders are very limited and you can be very frustrated trying to build your site using one of them.

What Are Web Hosting Companies Free Web Site Builders?

Web site builders are extremely useful for people who want to build a site yet have little or no knowledge of code (for example XHTML and PHP).

These days most Web hosting companies will include free Web site builders in your Web hosting package.

This is highly advantageous as site builders will provide you with the tools to assist you with the design and construction of your page and encourage you to build your own site without confusing you with complicated code.

What to Look For When Considering Site Builder Tools?

Consider what types of URLs the site builder creates, the number of pages you are allowed to make, the amount of versions of the site builder that you are entitled to in the package and the number and type of templates that are included with the site builder. It is also useful to check how much disk space and bandwidth you are allowed for building the Web site, especially if the site builder is part of a Web hosting package.

Also check the special features that come with the site builder, such as galleries, PayPal facilities, password protected areas and RSS capability.

What Do You Really Need?

I learned very early on that most people, like speakers, trainers, and authors, and most small organizations and businesses do not need a super exotic site that costs a lot of money to create and maintain.

Neither should it beyond the capabilities of the individual to at least maintain the site with updates, calendar changes, newsletters, and the like without resorting to outside help.

From a practical standpoint, a Web site has to be capable of supplying you with the ability to create a custom look, and allow you to put in enough text, graphics, and linking to make it worthwhile.

What's more, it shouldn't be so complicated that you have to take a course in HTML programming in order to use it which, incidentally, is what many of the *free* offers require.

After listening to a lot of feedback from our seminar attendees and reading a lot of reviews about how expensive and complex it was to create a simple Web site, we started doing research on what was going on and found that there are several places to create free Web sites that are not a scam in terms of their functionality as well as their ease of usage.

Of course, if the Web site doesn't do what you need it to do; it's not worth anything either so we set out with the following basic criteria understanding that the more exotic features could be added for a price:

No hosting fees
No software fees
Instruction manuals and video demos for all functions
Unique domain
Templates for basic site design
Ability to customize template design
Linked table of contents
Ability to create text and graphics pages
Ability to add a shopping cart like PayPal
Ability to link to other sites and pages
Ability to add custom HTML if desired

Since nothing is really free on the Web, that looked like a pretty tall order but we started looking and actually found places that will allow you to create your Web site with enough content to do you some good, for free.

In the process of our research, we found this YouTube video that reviews the top three sites. It's worth the five minute investment to see what's going on in the world off free Web sites. http://tinyurl.com/lsjj32k

Let's start with the Web design software itself and review what look for.

Feature Set

A successful Web site utilizes the best of Web 2.0 and the new Web 3.0 along with proven design elements. Good Web design software will include utilities for inserting links, images, tags and keywords.

It should also have multimedia support, e-commerce capabilities, and advanced features such as an HTML editor. Good Web design applications should also provide security measures such as site backup so it is possible to pull up previous versions of site in the case of a crash.

Templates

Good Web design software provides Web site templates that serve as a starting point for users. The templates should be professional, polished and easy to customize with your own content. Ideally, the software should offer you the ability to create your own design or to use additional templates that can be downloaded online.

Tet

Since there is a lot of text involved in a Web site, it's imperative that the software contain a robust text editing system that allows you to import text, generate text, and format the text. A desirable feature is the ability to preformat text using your own word processor and import it, as is, directly to the Web software.

Graphic Imaging Tools

Web design software should allow you to customize and enhance images for your site. You should be able to crop and resize and compress images directly in the software plus it should allow you to upload and use your own library of graphics, clip art and photographs.

Ease of Use

As a consumer or small business owners, you probably don't have, nor are you interested in, taking extensive training in Web design or scripting languages.

Therefore, to be effective, the Web design software should be easy to use, even for beginners. The ideal software is intuitive and provides the designer with a "what you see is what you get" (WYSIWG) working environment.

Help and Support

Given its technical and utilitarian function, Web design software should be supplemented with ample help and support options.

Most importantly, there should be a built-in help section that can be accessed directly (and printed out) in the software. Finally, a variety of online resources should also be offered including user forums, FAQs and how-to guides.

Whether developing a Web site for business, pleasure or both, be sure to read our in-depth reviews of the best Web design software on the market.

Wikipedia created an ongoing report that has resulted in a compressive report of the top ten free Web site systems.

A partial reprint of that chart is shown below but the complete information can be viewed from the Wikipedia site at http://tinyurl.com/laz9taf

You can look up each of these sites referenced using Google and judge for yourself what makes the most sense for both your needs and your technical capabilities.

Our Recommendations

After we tested over a dozen of the packages, we decided that www.Weebly.com had the best overall program. In fact, we actually created several free and fee sites for our own use as well as our clients. (Check out www.RoundsMiller.com and www.Clutterology.com It's COOL☺)

Weebly's well-organized interface makes it easy to see at a glance what it has to offer. It has a series of menus across the top for easy access to its key features. A simple drag and drop is all it takes to add text, images or forms to your Weebly Web site as you can see in the video.

Weebly's pricing

The Web site doesn't reveal too much about pricing. So here's the deal: the basic package is free, but will include a small Weebly ad in your Web site's footer.

The Pro plan will cost you a very reasonable USD $4.99 per month if you sign up two years. You get to the price list only after signing up for the free version, but an e-mail address is all it takes to register. Note that you will have to pay extra for your own domain name, however. A .com domain will be USD $39.95 per year (with discounts for longer terms).

Here's what we found:

Ease of use: This is exactly how a Web site builder should be. There's no learning curve with Weebly, so you'll have your Web site up and running in no time.

Template choice and flexibility: Range of attractive designs with access to the source code for customization. Also possible to use a template you've coded from scratch. A smart phone-friendly Web site will even be generated automatically.

Advertisement-free: Yes, but in the Pro version only. The free version has a small advertising link in the footer.

Languages: Currently available in English, French, Spanish, German, Italian and Chinese. Support available in English only. No special feature to create multilingual sites.

Features: Top-level domain (for example .com or .net). Yes you can buy a domain from Weebly, but they only offer .com, .net or .org domains. However, you can re-direct a domain you've bought elsewhere though.

Depth of navigation—Unlimited: A drop down menu is added to your navigation bar automatically.

Widgets (small tools to add extra functionality): Photo galleries, video and music players and more. We very much like the Button-Widget that let's you create call-to-action buttons easily.

Monetization (yes): Using Google Adsense or other banner ads.

e-Commerce: Simple store, but only accepts payments via PayPal or Google but does work with pay per download sites like E-Junkie.com.

Search-Engine Optimization (SEO): Title, meta and description tags are all customizable at page level, as are your images' ALT text. URL text is always created from the respective menu item.

BLOG: Has all the standard features, like comment moderation and trackbacks. Thanks to the iPhone app you can even BLOG on the go.

Visitor Statistics: Weebly has its own tracking tool, or you can use Google Analytics.

Contact Form: Use drag and drop to create detailed contact forms or surveys.

Add HTML code: Yes Allows you to add external widgets and other tools.

Storage Space Unlimited: Individually, your files cannot exceed 5 MB each on the free plan, or 100 MB each on the Pro plan. But other than that, the sky's the limit!

No limits on bandwidth either: And you can even download your Weebly Web site and host it on your own Web space.

Forums: Yes Direct integration with Tal.ki, which makes adding forums quick and easy.

Support: e-mail and tech support responded competently and quickly to our questions.

Fun factor: Weebly' s editor is one of the fastest out there, and it's very easy to use. Simply put, Weebly is a pleasure!

Overall rating: One of the best Web site builders on the market. There's room for improvement in its store, but other than that, Weebly hits the spot.

Conclusion

At first glance, the Weebly Web site seems nothing special. But take a closer look and you'll discover an outstanding tool. It's simple, uncluttered and easy to use, and that's exactly what people with limited technical skills need it comes to creating your own Internet presence.

Added to this, Weebly's price/performance ratio is one of the best on the market: you can build up to 10 completely separate Web sites on the Pro plan.

Please note that although the free plan will actually allow you to accomplish many of the e-commerce tasks, like creating a site to sell products and use PayPal for payment, it lacks the ability to add video (like promotional infomercials) and some other key features that are readily available at a reasonable price in the pro version.

Creating A Web Site Using Weebly.com

Weebly.com is a Web site where anyone with basic word processing skills can create a Web site at no cost. No special software is required and there are no hosting fees for the basic site and less than $5 bucks a month for your own domain name and all of the professional features you ever want or need.

Before starting, let's review some basic Web design tips.

To achieve a more professional look or style for your site, make sure you follow these rules:

Generally speaking, text should be left aligned. Titles may be centered.

Only links should be underlined. This is the convention of the Web . . . underlined text is a link. However, links do not have to be underlined. They may be bold or in a different color from the other text.

Use several short pages that can be accessed from the navigation bar rather than one long page. Most people do not like to do a lot of scrolling.

Content font size should be relatively small. Title font may be larger. The Weebly design you select will automatically provide you correctly sized fonts.

Use transparent graphics (such as a PNG) on a colored background. If this is not possible, the image will usually look better if given a thin border in black or grey.

Select a design that has a white or very pale background.
The amount of free help, tips, and useful processes for Weebly seems to be growing at an exponential rate.

We've included some great tutorial video links below but for an almost unlimited number of them, go to www.YouTube.com and type **Weebly Help** in the search box.

Trick to Re-Sizing Weebly Slideshow Element
http://tinyurl.com/k3x2nt3

How to Install and Modify YouTube Videos in Weebly
http://tinyurl.com/mhzrg57

How to Install New External Fonts in Weebly
http://tinyurl.com/mpt8lv8

How to Customize the Horizontal Divider in Weebly
http://tinyurl.com/mmyr64u

How to Set Up Side Column in Weebly
http://tinyurl.com/m3yg8wu

How to Export Weebly Web site and transfer into different host
http://tinyurl.com/kpoeym6

How to Delete Weebly Elements Efficiently
http://tinyurl.com/mc4gb2d

How to Change Header Images
http://tinyurl.com/mflp8ot

DivTag Weebly BLOG
http://tinyurl.com/kvlsq7b

Weebly also offers proprietary online training for free at http://tinyurl.com/67flgdr

To get started, point your Web browser to www.Weebly.com and sign up by inputting a username (your choice), password (again, your choice), and your e-mail address.

In the future, when you come back to work on the site, all you will need to do is log in using the box in the upper right corner of the page.

Now you are ready to create!! So, Click Create a Site, give your site a Title (which you can change at any time.)

For Type of Site, choose the one that's appropriate for your needs, click Continue and get going.

Weebly provides you with a 'walk through' that will help you to create your first site quickly and easily.

For additional help, including the instructions for using the features included in the Pro version, go to http://tinyurl.com/7t463px and type in your specific needs.

Last Thoughts

E-commerce isn't the holy grail of business but it is one of the most effective ways for individuals with limited budgets to start and operate a lucrative business for themselves.

The ability to offer goods and services domestically and internationally without having to maintain a huge inventory, rent a physical business location or warehouse, and making your offerings available 24 hours a day are just a few of the great reasons why e-commerce has exploded into the marketplace.

These days, most consumers shop online and the majority of those shoppers prefer shopping online for reasons like saving time and avoiding crowds.

The e-commerce junkies at *Invesp*™ put together the infographic below which looks at the sales volume associated with online shopping.

Ecommerce sales in the US are growing at a 19 percent per year and will reach $1.4 trillion by 2015
Europe is the second highest grossing e-commerce sales region (34 percent
Mobile e-commerce growth has steadily increased since 2009.

When you consider that sales are what drive the economy, it's no wonder that independent businesses everywhere are looking at the world of e-commerce as their primary source of income.

Whether you decide to enter the world of e-commerce on a full time or a part time business, know that you're in good company and that it's here to stay.

This manual includes a complete set of videos available that explain the mechanics of setting up a PayPal site, adding Pay per download, and a variety of other e-commerce functions.

Go to http://tinyurl.com/qj455c3 and use the password CPM7MFR

Rounds Miller and Associates

6318 Ridgepath Court
Rancho Palos Verdes, CA 90275-3248
310.544.9502
www.RoundsMiller.com

Business, Technology and Organizing Training Specialists

PRODUCT CATALOG

Audio/Video Toolkit

Complete Windows® software series including: **Banner Maker** PDF with video instruction for making your own web site banner using Microsoft Publisher®; links and information for 100,000+ royalty free graphics, sources for free music for videos and slideshows. **CamStudio**™ Video Screen recording software. **VideoSoft**™ Complete audio/video editing and conversion suite including 55 separate conversion programs for video, audio, and mobile devices. **Audacity**™ Audio recording and editing software.

Audio/Data CD+ **$24.95**

Book Marketing for the Clueless®

Want to sell your books, CDs and DVDs for a profit? This audio/PDF CD includes databases of over 500 catalogs and outlets that market books and instructions on how to solicit your publications including how to be listed with Amazon.com for free.

Audio/Data CD+ ISBN 978-1-891440-49-6 **$24.95**
*eBook** ISBN 978-1-891440-94-6 **$9.95**

Business Training for the Clueless®

A complete course about becoming a six figure a year business trainer. Contains a complete PDF manual, workbook, training aids, exercise, games, on-screen timing software, and royalty free audio clips.

Book & Data CD+ ISBN 978-1-891440-85-4 **$69.95**
*eBook** ISBN 978-1-891440-96-0 **$9.95**

Cash From Your Clutter

A manual filled with resources to help you turn your excess stuff into cash. Includes information on what sells, where to sell your excess stuff, how to place a realistic sales value on your stuff, the best time to sell your stuff, how to donate for tax deductions, a special section on how to sell your timeshare property and much more.

*eBook** ISBN 978-1-891440-79-3 **$9.95**

The Clutter Bug Attacks Christmas Clutter™

If there's one time of the year our homes and lives become more cluttered, it's Christmas. Here are quick and easy ways to simplify Christmas, including how to: plan and organize your Christmas, get your card and gift lists under control, simplify your gift giving, handle the gifts you receive, and get rid of Christmas clutter!

Book ISBN 978-1-891440-74-8 **$15.95**
*eBook** ISBN 978-1-891440-84-7 **$9.95**

The Clutter Bug Attacks Junk Mail, Spam and Telemarketers™

Overwhelmed by Junk Mail? Spam? Telemarketers? These can all be stopped! Current, verified information with visual examples for quick and easy understanding. The first book ever to show you how to get off of political mailings, plus proven and structured processes for both eliminating and retaining communications.

*eBook** ISBN 978-1-891440-81-6 **$9.95**

eBooks contain a complete book in PDF for use on all Mac & Windows PCs, including desktops, notebooks/laptops, netbooks & tablets.
All data files are in PDF format, playable/viewable on Windows and Mac, audio files are in Wave format playable on standard CD players.

The Clutter Bug Investigates Coupons, Discounts, and Deals™

A complete manual describing the coupon process and how to use them to save 35 to 85 percent on you shopping. Includes complete detailed illustrations and examples on where to find coupons, types of coupons store policies for coupons, deals and discounts, rebates and refunds, and rewards and loyalty cards.

Book	ISBN 978-1-891440-77-9	*$24.95*
*eBook**	ISBN 978-1-891440-82-3	*$9.95*

Clutterology® Getting Rid of Clutter and Getting Organized! 4th Edition

Revised and Expanded! A complete manual on how to get organized, set up and maintain manageable filing sys tems, and eliminate clutter that gets in your way. Provides some of the simplest, easiest and most practical advic on how to remove the clutter from your life and get organized.

Book	ISBN 978-1-891440-89-2	*$34.9*
*eBook**	ISBN 978-1-891440-71-7	*$9.9*

Highlights of Clutterology®

This audio CD has over 60 minutes of tips, tricks, insights, and stories about getting rid of your clutter and gettin organized. It's ideal for reinforcement to remind you that getting organized is a step-by-step process that you ca accomplish if you take it easy and stick with it.

Audio CD+	ISBN 978-1-891440-44-1	*$19.9*

How to Become a Clutterologist™

Do label makers and shelf dividers make you smile? Use your aptitude for organization to change lives and tur your decluttering skills into a moneymaking career; become a professional organizer! Includes the tools an knowledge you need to succeed in the professional organizer industry: organizing specialties, understanding th Clutter-Hoarding Scale, how to structure your business for SUCCESS, business licensing and insurance.

Book	ISBN 978-1-891440-56-4	*$34.9*
*eBook**	ISBN 978-1-891440-68-7	*$9.9*

Consulting for the Clueless®

In today's business climate, consultants are flourishing while others can't find a job. This book will show you ho to profitably leverage your experience into a six-figure income with minimal investment. Includes DVD wit consulting seminar, PDF copy of Marketing the One-Person Business, and support software.

Book and Windows Software DVD *$39.9*

Contracts and Agreements for Inventors

Over a dozen of the most utilized agreements to help ensure that what's yours stays yours. With the help of a attorney, they contain everything you'll need from a confidentiality agreement to work-for-hire agreements, as signment of rights, and partnership agreements. Comes with instructions for usage, filling out, and filing whe applicable.

Data CD+ *$19.9*

E-Commerce for the Clueless®

Complete manual plus instruction program on CD that includes Flash® video on what e-commerce is and isn what's required to get involved, how to set up a web site page for e-commerce, setting up a FREE PayPal accou and product purchase buttons, and how to set up a pay-per-download account to sell e-books and other informatio products directly from your web site. Includes royalty free background music clips

Book	ISBN 978-1-891440-80-9	*$39.9*
Data CD+	ISBN 978-1-891440-78-6	*$24.9*

**eBooks contain a complete book in PDF for use on all Mac & Windows PCs, including desktops, notebooks/laptops, netbooks & table*
+All data files are in PDF format, playable/viewable on Windows and Mac, audio files are in Wave format playable on standard CD player

Fishin' With A Net, 8th Edition

Learn the elements of designing a Web site that actually works for you and can be created in less than four hours. Covers what the Web really is, what to put on your site to be successful, and how to link with the search engines quickly and easily.

Book ISBN 978-1-891440-97-7 ***$24.95***

Headline Creator™ Pro Suite

"Your headline can result in 80 percent or more of the effectiveness of your ad or sales page!" Automatically generates time-tested, proven, results-oriented headlines based on the greatest headlines in history. . . and does it in 17 seconds!

Windows Software CD+ ***$39.95***

How To Sell Your Inventions for Cash, 3rd Edition

Everything you need to know to be a successful inventor! Takes your idea from inception through the licensing process to a manufacturer for royalties. Learn how to protect your inventions using patents, trademarks, copyrights, and other legal instruments, determine if you're ready to offer your idea, and how to find and solicit manufacturers who are interested in your ideas.

Book ISBN 978-1-891440-59-5 ***$24.95***
*eBook** ISBN 978-1-891440-63-2 ***$9.95***
Audio CD+ ISBN 978-1-891440-28-1 ***$39.95***

Intellectual Property Protection for the Clueless®

CD contains 3 hours of audio plus 100s of pages in PDF format on trademarks, patents and copyright. Includes forms for filing without an attorney! *Bonus: How to Apply for an Innovation Research Grant!* This audio is in MP3 format playable with the Windows Media Player or comparable MP3 software.

MP3 Audio/Data CD+ ISBN 978-1-891440-67-0 ***$59.95***

Marketing the One-Person Business, 2nd Edition

A one-person business is different from any other because you have to do the business PLUS get the business. Contains complete information about setup, operation, independent contractor criteria and forms, fee setting, consulting, public speaking, seminars, contracts and agreements.

Book ISBN 978-1-891440-29-8 ***$24.95***
*eBook** ISBN 978-1-891440-88-5 ***$9.95***

Mechanics of Starting a Home-Based Business, 2nd Edition

A home-based business is a business whose primary office is in the owner's home. Explains the realities of starting and operating a home business and including resources for taxes, licenses, and advertising plus computer operated business you can start and run.

Book ISBN 978-1-891440-64-9 ***$34.95***
*eBook** ISBN 978-1-891440-70-0 ***$9.95***

Photo Manipulator Software

Shrink Pic™ software automatically reduces the size of photos for email, blogging and web galleries. No set up, no operating instructions, just send your photos normally and Shrink Pic™ does the work. Paint Shop Pro™ 4 is an easy to use photo editing program that let's you enhance your photos and create professional-looking images.

Windows Software CD+ ***$19.95***

Professional Speaking for the Clueless®

Do you want to be paid to speak? This book explains the REAL business of professional speaking and how to make six figures a year without huge marketing and advertising costs. Includes dozens of resources, databases, and complete explanations of how to locate speaking opportunities and market to them.

Audio/Data CD+ ISBN 978-1-891440-53-3 ***$24.95***
*eBook** ISBN 978-1-891440-91-5 ***$9.95***

**eBooks contain a complete book in PDF for use on all Mac & Windows PCs, including desktops, notebooks/laptops, netbooks & tablets.*
+All data files are in PDF format, playable/viewable on Windows and Mac, audio files are in Wave format playable on standard CD players.

Profitable Publishing for the Clueless®

The complete 3 CD set containing everything you need to know to generate, protect, and market your printed work. See full description for each item.

Disk 1 - Self-Publishing for the Clueless®
Disk 2 - Trademarks & Copyrights for the Clueless®
Disk 3 - Book Marketing for the Clueless®

Audio/Data CD+ ISBN 978-1-891440-51-9 **$59.95**

Project Management for the Clueless®

Zipped file containing a 1-hour audio seminar and all of the documents you'll need to organize, plan and budget most projects in three hours or less.

*eBook** ISBN 978-1-891440-95-3 **$9.95**

Self-Publishing for the Clueless®, 2nd Edition

Complete workbook on self-publishing, e-publishing, and a secured access to a 270 page manual with the latest information, resources, and insider tips about the world of e-publishing including how to be e-published in a week.

Workbook and Data CD+ ISBN 978-1-891440-99-1 **$34.95**

Trademarks & Copyrights for the Clueless®

Trademarks are the mark of your trade and copyrights address the laws allowing you the rights to make copies of your work. Contains printable forms and examples, explaining how to protect your works plus what material of others you can use without fear of legal problems.

Audio/Data CD+ ISBN 978-1-891440-30-4 **$24.95**
*eBook** ISBN 978-1-891440-92-2 **$9.95**

Venture Capital for the Clueless®

Venture Capital is available for all types of businesses and your ability to tap into it depends on your ability to write a business plan that sells you and your ideas to the people with the money. Includes explanations, samples, printable forms, and sources of venture funding.

Audio/Data CD+ ISBN 978-1-891440-31-1 **$24.95**
*eBook** ISBN 978-1-891440-93-9 **$9.95**

Virtual Business for the Clueless®

Use the Latest Technology to Improve Business, Sales, and Communications. Computers have given us virtual tools that you can use to improve your productivity, whether you are a volunteer organization, a small business or a large enterprise. Covers: PowerPoint Programs - Beyond the Basics; Audio and Video Podcasts, Tele-Seminars and Webinars; Green Screen and On-Demand Programming; and more!

Book ISBN 978-1-891440-63-2 **$39.95**

Whadda We Do NOW?™

Provides quick fixes for failing businesses. Learn how to quickly and easily figure out what's wrong so you can stop guessing and start implementing solutions. The information is practical, easy to understand, and readily implementable if you're serious about getting your business into a positive cash flow position-NOW!

Book ISBN 978-1-891440-66-3 **$29.95**

**eBooks contain a complete book in PDF for use on all Mac & Windows PCs, including desktops, notebooks/laptops, netbooks & tablets*
+All data files are in PDF format, playable/viewable on Windows and Mac, audio files are in Wave format playable on standard CD players

Training Kits

Become a Professional Organizer

If you'd like to get into the lucrative world of professional organizing, then everything you'll need to setup a business, get clients, and operate profitably is on the list below. Contains:

Books: How to Become a Clutterologist™, Clutterology® Getting Rid of Clutter and Getting Organized!; Fishin' with a Net™, How to Develop an Effective Web Site; Mechanics of Starting a Home-Based Business™, and Self-Publishing for the Clueless® 2nd edition

Plus DVD/CDs: Headline Creator™ Pro Suite, Marketing the One-Person Business™, and Highlights of Clutterology©

Kit $261.95

Entrepreneurship

Do you dream of working for yourself? This kit includes everything for setting up a home-based business, getting organized, raising venture capital to fund the efforts, scheduling and managing your time, and ways to market your skills profitably.

Contains: Books: Mechanics of Starting a Home-Based Business™, Clutterology® Getting Rid of Clutter and Getting Organized!, Fishin' with a Net™, How to Develop an Effective Web Site, and Self-Publishing for the Clueless® 2nd edition.

Plus DVD/CDs: Marketing the One-Person Business™, Headline Creator™ Pro Suite, Professional Speaking for the Clueless®, and Venture Capital for the Clueless®.

Kit $169.95

Invention Marketing

The material listed is endorsed by the SBA as "The only legitimate program for marketing inventions that we've ever seen." It explains how to organize and manage your invention process, protect them with patents, trademarks and copyrights, set up a home business, offer your ideas for sale, plus information for raising venture capital to fund your projects.

Contains: Books: How to Sell Your Inventions for Cash™ and Mechanics of Starting a Home-Based Business.

Plus DVD/CDs: How to Sell Your Inventions for Cash, Contracts and Agreements for Inventors, Venture Capital for the Clueless®, and Trademarks & Copyrights for the Clueless®.

Kit $161.95

Professional Speaking

If you're interested in professional speaking, you'll find everything needed to get profitable bookings including places to get booked and instructions on how to do it! Includes over 1,700 pages of printable information, eight hours of video, four hours of audio, and hundreds of support resources.

Contains: Books: Mining the College Market, Mechanics of Starting A Home-Based Business, and Fishin' with a Net™, How to Develop an Effective Web Site, Self-Publishing for the Clueless® 2nd edition, and Business Training for the Clueless® (plus CDs),

Plus DVD/CDs: Headline Creator™ Pro Suite, Marketing the One-Person Business, Professional Speaking for the Clueless®.

Kit $461.95

Raising Venture Capital

Looking for money or backing for a new idea or enterprise? Confused about what to do and how to approach investors? We've assembled the materials needed to establish proprietary rights to your innovations; plan, budget, organize and schedule your project; prepare a business plan and shop it to people with investment capital. Contains:

Books: Clutterology® Getting Rid of Clutter and Getting Organized! and Mechanics of Starting a Home-Based Business, Fishin' with a Net™, How to Develop an Effective Web Site, and Self-Publishing for the Clueless® 2nd Edition.

Plus DVD/CDs: Trademarks & Copyrights for the Clueless®, Venture Capital for the Clueless®, Headline Creator™ Pro Suite, and Highlights of Clutterology©.

Kit $191.95

eBooks contain a complete book in PDF for use on all Mac & Windows PCs, including desktops, notebooks/laptops, netbooks & tablets. All data files are in PDF format, playable/viewable on Windows and Mac, audio files are in Wave format playable on standard CD players.

Self-Publishing

You CAN have a book ready to sell in 30 days with these practical products. . . guaranteed! Contains everything needed including pre-configured scheduling and budgeting charts to get your own project finished in record time with a minimal amount of expense and hassles.

Contains: Books: Mechanics of Starting A Home-Based Business, Fishin' with a Net™, How to Develop an Effective Web Site, and Self-Publishing for the Clueless® 2nd edition.

Plus DVD/CDs: Trademarks & Copyrights for the Clueless®, Book Marketing for the Clueless®, and Headline Creator™ Pro Suite.

Kit $261.95

Web Site Development Software Suite

No software you use to create your Web site will contain everything you need, so we've assembled the "stuff they left out." This suite of software and resources will help make your Web site work efficiently and get the response it deserves. These products have a proven track record in the world of Web design, marketing and advertising.

Contains: DVD/CDs: AV Toolkit; Photo Manipulator Toolkit, Headline Creator™ Pro Suite, Trademarks & Copyrights for the Clueless®, and E-Commerce for the Clueless®.

Kit $100.00

**eBooks contain a complete book in PDF for use on all Mac & Windows PCs, including desktops, notebooks/laptops, netbooks & tablet*
+All data files are in PDF format, playable/viewable on Windows and Mac, audio files are in Wave format playable on standard CD player

Rounds Miller and Associates

6318 Ridgepath Court
Rancho Palos Verdes, CA 90275-3248
310.544.9502
www.RoundsMiller.com

Business, Technology and Organizing Training Specialists

ORDER FORM

ITEM (See Catalog for Full Description)	Format	Qty.	Price
Audio/Video Toolkit	Audio/Data CD $24.95		
Book Marketing for the Clueless®	Audio/Data CD $24.95		
	eBook - Online $9.95	PURCHASE ONLINE	
Business Training for the Clueless®	Book & Data CD $69.95		
	eBook - Online $9.95	PURCHASE ONLINE	
Cash From Your Clutter	eBook - Online $9.95	PURCHASE ONLINE	
The Clutter Bug Attacks Christmas Clutter™	Book $15.95		
	eBook - Online $9.95	PURCHASE ONLINE	
The Clutter Bug Attacks Junk Mail, Spam and Telemarketers™	eBook - Online $9.95	PURCHASE ONLINE	
The Clutter Bug Investigates Coupons, Discounts, and Deals™	Book $24.95		
	eBook - Online $9.95	PURCHASE ONLINE	
Clutterology® Getting Rid of Clutter and Getting Organized!	Book $34.95		
	eBook - Online $9.95	PURCHASE ONLINE	
Highlights of Clutterology®	Audio CD $19.95		
How to Become a Clutterologist™	Book $34.95		
	eBook - Online $9.95	PURCHASE ONLINE	
Consulting for the Clueless®	Book/Software DVD $39.95		
Contracts and Agreements for Inventors	Data CD $19.95		
E-Commerce for the Clueless®	Data CD $24.95		
	Book $24.95		
Fishin' With A Net	Book $24.95		
Headline Creator™ Pro Suite	Software CD $39.95		
How To Sell Your Inventions for Cash	Book $24.95		
	eBook - Online $9.95	PURCHASE ONLINE	
	Audio CD $39.95		
Intellectual Property Protection for the Clueless®	MP3 Audio/Data CD $59.95		
Marketing the One-Person Business	Book $24.95		
	eBook - Online $9.95	PURCHASE ONLINE	
Mechanics of Starting a Home-Based Business	Book $34.95		
	eBook - Online $9.95	PURCHASE ONLINE	
Photo Manipulator Software	Software CD $19.95		
Professional Speaking for the Clueless®	Audio/Data CD $24.95		
	eBook - Online $9.95	PURCHASE ONLINE	
Profitable Publishing for the Clueless®	3 Audio/Data CDs $59.95		
Project Management for the Clueless®	eBook - Online $9.95	PURCHASE ONLINE	
Self-Publishing for the Clueless®	Workbook & Data CD $34.95		

Page 1 Sub-Total	

Trademarks & Copyrights for the Clueless®	*Audio/Data CD $24.95*		
	eBook - Online $9.95	PURCHASE ONLINE	
Venture Capital for the Clueless®	*Audio/Data CD $24.95*		
	eBook - Online $9.95	PURCHASE ONLINE	
Virtual Business for the Clueless®	*Book $39.95*		
Whadda We Do NOW?™	*Book $29.95*		
TRAINING KITS			
Become a Professional Organizer	*Kit $261.95*		
Entrepreneurship	*Kit $169.95*		
Invention Marketing	*Kit $161.95*		
Professional Speaking	*Kit $461.95*		
Raising Venture Capital	*Kit $191.95*		
Self-Publishing	*Kit $261.95*		
Web Site Development Software Suite	*Kit $100.00*		

E-Books are available for purchase and instant download online at www.RMACart.com/E-Books.htm

Amount from Page 1	
Sub-Total	
in CA add Sales Tax 9.75%	
Shipping	**$2.95**
Total	

Thank You!

Name (please print) ______________________________

Mailing Address: ______________________________

City, State, ZIP: ______________________________

Tel: ____________________ e-Mail: ____________________

I authorize Rounds, Miller and Associates to charge my credit card for the items listed above

VISA | AMERICAN EXPRESS Cards | MasterCard | DISCOVER NOVUS

Credit Card Number: ____________________ exp. __________ CSS __________

Signature: ______________________________ Date: __________

To Order By Mail:

Send completed order form and check payable to Rounds, Miller and Associates to

6318 Ridgepath Court

Rancho Palos Verdes, CA 90275

View our entire product line at www.RoundsMiller.com

Printed in Dunstable, United Kingdom

91335487R00071